Anthony Swofford served in a U.S. Marine Corps Surveillance and Target Acquisition/Scout-Sniper Platoon during the Gulf War. After the war, he was educated at American River College; the University of California, Davis; and the University of Iowa Writers' Workshop. He has taught at the University of Iowa and Lewis and Clark College. His fiction and nonfiction have appeared in *The New York Times, Harper's, Men's Journal*, *The Iowa Review, NOON,* and other publications. A Michener-Copernicus Fellowship recipient, he lives in Portland, Oregon. He is at work on a novel.

THE NEW NORMAL

PORTFOLIO

THE NEW NORMAL

Great Opportunities in a Time of Great Risk

Roger McNamee

with David Diamond

PORTFOLIO
Published by the Penguin Group
Penguin Group (USA) Inc., 375 Hudson Street, New York, New York 10014, U.S.A.
Penguin Group (Canada), 10 Alcorn Avenue, Toronto, Ontario, Canada M4V 3B2 (a division of Pearson Penguin Canada Inc.) • Penguin Books Ltd, 80 Strand, London WC2R 0RL, England • Penguin Ireland, 25 St. Stephen's Green, Dublin 2, Ireland (a division of Penguin Books Ltd) • Penguin Books Australia Ltd, 250 Camberwell Road, Camberwell, Victoria 3124 Australia (a division of Pearson Australia Group Pty Ltd) • Penguin Books India Pvt Ltd, 11 Community Centre, Panchsheel Park, New Delhi – 110 017, India • Penguin Group (NZ), Cnr Airborne and Rosedale Roads, Albany, Auckland, New Zealand (a division of Pearson New Zealand Ltd) • Penguin Books (South Africa) (Pty) Ltd, 24 Sturdee Avenue, Rosebank, Johannesburg 2196, South Africa

Penguin Books Ltd, Registered Offices:
80 Strand, London WC2R 0RL, England

First published in 2004 by Portfolio,
a member of Penguin Group (USA) Inc.

10 9 8 7 6 5 4 3 2 1

PUBLISHER'S NOTE
This publication is designed to provide accurate and authoritative information in regard to the subject matter covered. It is sold with the understanding that the publisher is not engaged in rendering legal, accounting or other professional services. If you require legal advice or other expert assistance, you should seek the services of a competent professional.

LIBRARY OF CONGRESS CATALOGING IN PUBLICATION DATA
McNamee, Roger.
The new normal : great opportunities in a time of great risk / Roger McNamee with David Diamond.
p. cm.
Includes index.
ISBN 1-59184-059-7
1. Finance, Personal—United States. 2. Risk—United States. I. Diamond, David.
HG181.M385 2004
332.024—dc22 2004057269

This book is printed on acid-free paper. ♾

Printed in the United States of America
Designed by Jennifer Daddio

To Ann

ACKNOWLEDGMENTS

This book could not have happened without the contributions of many people. The idea began in response to a request from *Fast Company* magazine in November 2002, which asked me—as one of a couple dozen people—to write a paragraph or two about what might be the biggest issue facing the technology industry in 2003. It was the first time I described the New Normal in print. *Fast Company* liked the idea of the New Normal enough to dedicate its May 2003 issue to the subject, and I want to thank *Fast Company*'s Polly Labarre for that.

The book itself was the brainchild of Kelli Jerome, a miracle worker who masquerades as an agent. Kelli saw the New Normal issue of *Fast Company* and convinced me that it should be a book. Kelli doesn't advertise it, but she is also a terrific editor, and her guidance made this a better book than it would have been without her.

My editor, Adrian Zackheim, was the first person Kelli spoke to about *The New Normal.* He liked the idea from the beginning, gave me the courage to write a book, and motivated me throughout the project. For a guy with several day jobs and a night job, such motivation was really important. Without Adrian, the book would never have happened. Stephanie Land at Portfolio answered my pleas for help, providing editorial feedback when I needed it. My thanks also go to Will Weisser, Sarah Mollo-Christensen, and the rest of the incredible team at Portfolio for their guidance and support.

Adrian also introduced me to my writing partner, David Diamond. Blessed with the patience of a saint, as well as the ability to adopt—and refine—another's voice and style, David spent more than six months with me. He even did a minitour with the band!

Many friends and business partners contributed their time and energy to help bring *The New Normal* to fruition. My Elevation partners, Marc Bodnick, John Riccitiello, Fred Anderson, Bret Pearlman, and Bono, were unbelievably supportive, allowing me to write a book even as we created our new business. Marc read many chapters as we traveled back and forth to Europe, providing invaluable feedback. Carol Weston helped me relate the New Normal to families and education. Katrina Roche refined my thinking about how enterprises will use Web services. Karen Heller took a red pen to the first chapter, giving it focus. To these dear friends and everyone else who read chapters and provided moral support, I extend my thanks. You have made this a better book.

Adam Hopkins led the research team, which included Larry Aller, Ada Au Cheng, and Charles Dean. All four were students at the Stanford Graduate School of Business during this project, where they uncovered key anecdotes and statistics for this book. Adam, who worked with me at Silver Lake prior to business school, is a founding member of the team at Elevation.

My mother, Barbara Dudley, has encouraged me for years—sometimes subtly, sometimes not so subtly—to write a book. Thank you for not giving up on me. To Ann, my wife and partner of twenty-one years, I give the biggest thank-you of all. A woman of many talents, Ann is a master critic and copy editor.

While credit for *The New Normal* goes to these dear friends and everyone else who provided moral support, the responsibility for whatever shortcomings this book may have is mine alone.

CONTENTS

PART ONE: REALITY CHECK

PART TWO: A ROAD MAP THROUGH THE NEW NORMAL

INTRODUCTION: FOUR SECRETS OF THE NEW NORMAL

Remember the way everybody around the planet greeted the turn of the new millennium? From the coast of New Zealand to Hawaii's shores, culture after culture greeted a new day as a new beginning. We sipped champagne and gazed at our TV screens, holding hands and taking in the wonder of it all. It was more than just relief that the computers were still working and the Y2K fuss was behind us. This was a new day with promise. We couldn't help but feel a warm, optimistic glow.

Which lasted not quite three months. You know what happened next. The stock market collapsed and we couldn't figure out how to reboot. A band of terrorists sent our world tumbling. CEOs were caught cheating. Talk-show hosts were caught popping pills. Mutual fund firms abused their investors. Our nation went to war. Good friends lost their jobs and moved to some part of the country where there isn't a professional baseball team. Suddenly we struggle to put our shoes back on in the airport security line, while trying to figure out how it all took such a quick and messy fall. This isn't what we expected. This isn't what we were promised. And what's worse, it's hard to figure out when everything will turn itself around.

Look again. The future is already here. It's called the New Normal. New because everything from our perception of time to our advantages in making investment decisions to our ability to compete globally has changed. Normal because this altered landscape will be with us for a long time—at least for the coming decade.

At first glance, the world is a frightening place. The institutions that protected us no longer can. The safety nets that were strung up by government or corporations and supported previous generations have come unstitched. But there's a flip side to all the uncertainty.

The New Normal is a time of unlimited opportunities lurking in places we never bothered to look. Safety nets have been replaced by new possibilities. Corporate paternalism has been replaced by personal responsibility, which exposes us to more risk but also exposes us to more rewards. Technology and globalization have cleared a path for advancement that's right there under your feet—if you're willing to take the first step. The rewards have never been greater for those who act. But many are reluctant to act for fear of the unknown.

I see this everywhere. By day, I'm an investor whose livelihood depends on being able to ferret out the truth and being able to distinguish between the right opportunity and the almost right opportunity. By night, I play guitar in a rock 'n' roll band that tours the country, performing gigs in clubs and music festivals. From Palmer, Alaska, to Fort Lauderdale, Florida. From Tempe, Arizona, to Woodstock, New York. I have seen the cities and small towns of America—dozens of them in the past year alone—from the seat of a van and a room at a Best Western. I split my time between two worlds—Silicon Valley and Main Street—each of which is caught up in the New Normal.

What I've come to believe: more than anything else, the New Normal will reward the brave. As we already know too well, this is not your father's economy, where a corporation and your government provided a lifetime's worth of security. In the New Normal, you'll continually have to decide on things that, in the past, were decided for you, everything from how to keep your job to where to invest your retirement plan. The reward is that you will be in charge of your life. Truly in charge.

When your traditional sources of support don't provide the answers, it's time to start thinking for yourself—and to have the courage to be different. It's easier than you think.

Get ready for the rest of your life.

TIMES HAVE CHANGED—TAKE CHARGE OF YOUR WORLD

There are a lot of people out there who would have you believe the world is spinning out of control.

It may *feel* like the world is spinning out of control.

For some of us, the world may actually *be* spinning out of control.

When the Internet boom turned into a bust, when the recession hit, when terrorists struck, we were all caught off guard. The natural reaction was to focus on what wasn't working right. People were losing their jobs. Investments were losing value hand over fist. We came face-to-face with insecurity in far too many dimensions of our lives. It felt as though there was no way to call a timeout or to pursue a more productive path.

Fortunately, the free fall is over. No matter what anyone tells you, good things are happening for many people. Many more than you may realize. I don't pretend that the world is perfect, but it's a much better place than you might think if you believe everything you read, hear, or see in the media. And good things can happen for you. The trick is to know how to make them happen. It's time to think clearly about what's going on today. And about the future that lies ahead of you. It's time to figure out who and what you want to be, and put yourself on the right path.

I've been there. In the summer of 2001, as a healthy forty-five year old, I had a stroke. Two weeks later, I had open-heart surgery to repair a birth defect the doctors discovered as the cause of the stroke. My life was turned upside down. It took six months to get my body back to normal, and longer for everything else. Still mending, my first day back to work was September 11. One of my partners lost a brother in one of the planes, and just about every other partner at my firm was stuck overseas, requiring me to get right back into my normal world . . . normal, but not!

Within months my health was better than ever, but the world of technology investing had turned brutal. I seized the opportunity to rethink my goals and my future. As part of the process, I developed an understanding of the new environment we find ourselves in. Because I am an investor, and my job is to understand how trends affect the future, I also devoted a great deal of time to figuring out how the New Normal is likely to evolve over the coming decade, and what we need to know if we are to flourish in this era.

THE FOUR SECRETS OF THE NEW NORMAL

When it comes to the economy, too often the pundits are just plain wrong. What we really need is the economic equivalent of the

North Star, a fixed object in space that we can use to navigate the New Normal.

These secrets of the New Normal can be your North Star:

- The power of the individual is rising rapidly.
- The world offers more choices than ever, but it also requires us to make more decisions.
- Technology and globalization are facts of life; they rule our economy and they aren't going away.
- None of us has enough time, so making the most of the time we have is essential.

Helping you master these secrets is what this book is all about. Before you are done, you will more clearly understand why technology and globalization are so increasingly important, and you will have a better idea of what to do about them. You will also have perspective on what you can do to make your life better, to make the most of the opportunities and time available to you. Along the way, I also will include occasional Investor Alerts that will show you how to apply what you learn to personal investments.

THE RISE OF THE INDIVIDUAL

Our initial focus will be on the first secret, the power inherent in the rise of the individual. In the Old Normal, most people were part of an infrastructure that enabled them to spend a lot of time on autopilot. Life didn't require continual assessment. It was stable. When people took a job, they were fairly certain it would still be there as long as they wanted to stick around—assuming they performed reasonably well. There never was a suspicion that the job—or corporation or division—would evaporate or substantially change.

You could depend on it being there in a year. Five years. Fifteen years. And when troubles arose, you could rely on your boss or a trusted coworker to help you navigate. *Hey! Where'd they go?*

Today our economy has reinvented itself into something that would have been unimaginable a few decades ago. Decentralized, no-frills corporations dominate the economy. Governments have been forced to accept a lesser role in our lives. But this economic transformation has delivered something that most people have failed to either notice or leverage: power has shifted from institutions to individuals. When I say "individuals," I mean people just like you. Once again the fundamental building blocks of our economy, individuals have never been such a compelling economic force in the financial world. The rise in the influence of individuals, which I explain in detail throughout the book, can be daunting, as well as empowering. It rewards positive thinking and self-awareness. It rewards action.

In the New Normal, opportunities for success are plentiful. The trouble is, those opportunities are often different from the ones we are accustomed to. To exploit them, we have to think in new ways about ourselves and about the future. We have to get comfortable with change. We have to be self-confident. And we have to be prepared to step away from the crowd, understand how the situation relates to us, and act accordingly. Understanding the situation requires a balance between short-term and long-term objectives and intellectual honesty about our progress. There will be times when we should just get back in the saddle after a setback. In other cases, though, the best strategy is to change direction. We alone have to live with the consequences of our actions, so we should not let others make our choices for us.

Here's what I mean. Every community has conventional wisdom, which reflects the experience of past generations. While valuable for some people in some settings, conventional wisdom has important limitations. Sometimes you just have to ignore it. When my wife, Ann, was growing up, girls in her town rarely went to top-tier colleges, and none had ever become a professor. Ann's guidance counselors gave her terrible advice, based on conventional wisdom. Fortunately, Ann paid no attention. She graduated from Wellesley College, got a PhD from Yale, and enjoyed a long career as a professor at Swarthmore College. If you want to have a successful career in the New Normal, you need to understand how your own situation differs from the conventional wisdom. You should always balance immediate benefits—compensation and location, for example—with such long-term factors as career path and cultural fit. When it comes to career planning, no group is more predictably short term in its thinking than business school students. Most of them want to pursue a career in whatever sector is hot right now. For a while it was the Internet. Now it's private equity. For some, that choice makes sense. For most, it merely reflects business school groupthink. Most careers last decades, if not a lifetime. They should be chosen carefully, after a thorough analysis of one's personal strengths and interests and in conjunction with other factors.

As I said earlier, in the New Normal, more than at any previous time, it's important to know who you are and what you want. Take the time to clearly understand what motivates you. Be explicit about your long-term goals, and be realistic about the amount of work necessary to achieve them. Self-awareness is more critical today than it was in the past because you don't have institutions with time-tested game plans to fall back on. Today, you have to be self-reliant.

The upheavals in corporate America have left enterprises in a continuing state of change. To be successful, you have to be able to change, too. Flexibility has become a mantra in corporate America, but it is as important for individuals as it is for corporations. If you know who you are and what your goals are, you can adapt effectively to whatever situations arise. You will be able to leverage your successes and convert your setbacks into a valuable foundation for future success. In the New Normal, you can thrive, but you have to be able to think on your feet.

This book will explain the present as it helps you position yourself for the future. I will explore how technology and globalization have transformed the economy. I will help you set priorities that enable you to take advantage of the myriad of opportunities that are the heritage of the Internet boom.

THE NEW REALITY OF CHOICE

Another secret of the New Normal is that we live in a world of seemingly unlimited choices . . . and limited safety nets. It's easy to be seduced—and bewildered—by all the options. Making the most of the New Normal requires separating myth from reality.

Myth: Wall Street has never been more corrupt.
Reality: Individual investors have never had so much power.

Myth: Technology's heyday is over.
Reality: Technology's heyday is just beginning.

Myth: Businesses have less need for people.
Reality: Businesses depend on individuals more than ever before.

Myth: You should wait until a technology is proven before purchasing it for yourself or your company.
Reality: The true benefits will accrue to those who experiment with emerging technologies.

Myth: Wall Street is unrelentingly impatient and shortsighted.
Reality: Wall Street can be patient when the incentives justify patience.

Myth: Large companies have all the advantages.
Reality: Scale matters less now than at any time in memory.

Myth: All the best business ideas have been taken.
Reality: Don't get me started. . . .

Above all, the reality is this: we have more options than ever, sometimes more than we know how to handle. Faced with a deluge of choice, we have to make innumerable decisions. Only a handful of these decisions really matter. The rest are not worth worrying about. Part of my inspiration for writing this book was seeing so many of my friends paralyzed when it came to making decisions. They were out of work or in jobs they hated, unable to see the opportunities out there, much less act on them. Even if things at work were going well, they were inundated with choices on other fronts. Focus your energy on the important decisions, the ones related to family and career. Be decisive. Inaction is not a good option.

Have you ever wondered how some people manage to deal with a zillion things at once? Preparation. They get ready beforehand. To make thoughtful decisions, you need time. The best way to get enough time is to plan ahead. And if you're going to plan ahead, you might as well make the most of it and plan for the long haul. When making plans for your family, career, or investments, how far into the future do you plan? As I say in the chapter devoted to time: the people with the longest time horizon generally end up winning.

The New Normal will be with us for years, so you might as well make the best of it. Get to know yourself better. Figure out what you really want out of life. Set your priorities. Develop a framework for decision making. If you do, you will make better decisions faster and reduce your stress.

TECHNOLOGY + GLOBALIZATION = OPPORTUNITIES

The third secret of the New Normal can be found in its foundation: technology and globalization. Whether you like it or not, technology and globalization are here to stay. The good news is that both are generating an unprecedented volume of opportunities. Technology empowers individuals as never before. It lowers the barriers for small businesses, and gives individuals new tools for coping with a rapidly changing environment. It puts people more readily in touch with opportunities and with the people that matter in their lives.

Before the New Normal, the focus of technology was mostly on computation and keeping track of stuff. In those days, technology addressed clerical needs, analytical needs, and accounting needs. Now technology is about *doing* stuff. It's about the real world. Where technology used to just track how we spent our time and money, now it is the environment in which we actually *spend* our time and money. Technology has moved out of the workplace and into our lives. Everywhere we go, technology is there. In the old model, Nielsen ratings tracked what we watched on television. In the New Normal, technology affects how and what we watch on television. Technology enables television to be a platform for a wide range of entertainment choices: cable, DVD, TiVo, video games. And that's just television. We also have amazing consumer platforms in cellular phones and personal computers.

Meanwhile, there's globalization. You have a stake in making globalization succeed. Globalization increases standards of living—for us and for our country's trading partners—while simultaneously lowering costs and providing new markets for American goods and services.

The politicians and pundits who are inciting hysteria over the outsourcing of jobs to China are forgetting their macroeconomics. And their history. We've seen this movie many, many times before. A country—this time it's China—focuses its energy on economic development, builds infrastructure, and here's what inevitably happens. They export like crazy for a while. Then standards of living start rising in their country. Consumers buy stuff. They like what they buy, and soon they demand higher salaries to pay for more stuff. Before long, the emerging country's labor costs reach some kind of equilibrium relative to its trading partners. That's how macroeconomics works. It happened in Japan. It happened in Korea. It happened in Taiwan. It happened in Hong Kong. It happened in Singapore. It's happening in Thailand. It will happen in China and India.

When the economy is weak—as it has been until recently—people fear that the exporting of jobs just goes on forever. That is an understandable fear. It is the same logic many applied with respect to Japan in the 1980s. To say they were wrong about that would be a gross understatement. Remember Japan? Actually, the hysteria over Japan may have been worse than the hysteria around China, if only because some of the Japanese companies were so big and so overconfident. I'll never forget hearing a senior executive from Toshiba in the late 1980s explain how his company was going to use memory chips to crush the U.S. technology industry. I was intimidated. The panic over Japan seemed to increase right up until the last day of 1989, when Japan peaked for all time and promptly collapsed. It has never recovered. American companies once again dominate most segments of the computer and software industry. And a Korean company now dominates the market for memory chips.

You know what? Japan, Korea, Taiwan, Hong Kong, Singapore, Malaysia, Thailand—none of these countries destroyed the U.S. economy. In fact, their success *helped* our economy. It helped us adapt and grow stronger. Rising disposable income in those countries created demand for American products and made the world more stable. Stability is an important contributor to peace and security. It's when a country doesn't participate, like Indonesia, that it becomes really unstable.

TIME IS ALL AROUND YOU

The fourth and final secret to the New Normal relates to time. The New Normal revives the less frantic notion of time that prevailed prior to the Internet mania, but with a twist. Time has slowed to a normal pace, but there is so much more going on in our lives that most of us feel overwhelmed some or all the time. The trick is to use the other New Normal levers—technology, for example—to make the most of the time you have.

Time ties together the other secrets of the New Normal. The levers of individuality, choice, technology, and globalization have their own power, but success comes from optimizing their interaction with time.

What separates New Normal winners from losers is how the former approach time. Do you use time as a lever, or is it a force that constrains you? Armed with this book, you can find time for everything that really matters to you. That's what New Normal winners do. They break away from the pack to set a unique course, balancing work, family, and play, in both the short term and long term.

WHERE I'M COMING FROM

Throughout this book, I examine the growing opportunities brought to life by the New Normal. And I examine the range of new choices we face. You might wonder where I'm coming from—and how I came to develop my opinions and insights.

I'm a college history major whose life has had many ups and downs. I left Yale after my sophomore year and followed my girlfriend to the West Coast. (This was in the 1970s, when this sort of detour was relatively standard behavior.) If I wanted to eat, I needed a real job. I had been a reporter and copy editor at the *Yale Daily News,* and thought I would become an investigative journalist in the mode of Woodward and Bernstein. This was shortly after Watergate, when an entire generation woke up to the notion that journalists can change the world. Newspapers were flooded with job candidates. When I called the *San Francisco Chronicle* upon my arrival in California, the editor laughed at me and suggested I call their classified ad department and ask them for a job. Next, I called the weekly alternative newspaper, the *Bay Guardian.* The person there also laughed at me and suggested that I call their display ad department. Two calls in a matter of minutes, and my life changed forever.

I had never sold anything in my life, so I didn't realize how tricky it is to sell advertising space. It occurred to me that there was an inverse correlation between the publication size and the opportunity: the bigger the publication, the smaller the ads I could sell. That meant the *smallest* newspaper would offer the biggest prospect for responsibility, skills development, and earnings potential. That insight turned out to be right. I found myself selling ads for a biweekly, French-language newspaper in San Francisco. The newspaper was so small that I was the entire advertising department. I did everything from selling ads to creating artwork to collecting accounts receivable. I learned something that's probably obvious to many people: each new responsibility expands your mind, your perspective, and your skills. It multiplies your opportunities. I also learned how to judge people and businesses. When you both sell and collect, you learn quickly that there is no point in selling to a customer who can't or won't pay you.

Each morning before I went to work, I watched a television show about the stock market. At that point in my life—I was twenty years old—I knew nothing about investing. But every day, I watched the show. I started reading the *Wall Street Journal.* I read Benjamin Graham's *Intelligent Investor*. I started to learn about companies. I did some investment research. Eventually, I summoned the courage to buy a stock. It was Beech Aircraft, a maker of private airplanes. I bought a few shares at twenty dollars. A week later the stock jumped to twenty-six dollars and I thought I was the second coming of Jay Gould. I was hooked.

About a year after I moved to California, my father died. His death meant that I would have to earn a lot more of the money needed to complete my college degree. After thirty months in California, I had earned enough money to return to Yale. This was where I met Ann, who was completing her doctorate in music theory. I still needed more money than your average student job would pay, so I persuaded a repertory film society at Yale to let me create a magazine-style program—with pictures and descriptions of an entire semester's films—so that I would have a platform for selling advertisements. I split the net proceeds with the film society. That venture earned me enough money to finish college and go to business school at Dartmouth's Amos Tuck School. It was there that I discovered that you could have a career investing in stocks.

Unfortunately, I arrived at Tuck in the fall of 1980, when the stock market was weak and getting weaker. As I looked for a full-time job in my second year, a bear market was in full swing, and investment jobs were few and far between. Fortunately, only a handful of business school students that year were interested in stock-investing careers, so I was able to land a job with T. Rowe Price Associates. I started my career just as the bull market began in August 1982.

I found that I liked being an investor and had a personality well suited to the profession. I'm naturally curious, observant, and can dart easily between the minute details and the big picture. More than almost anything else, I enjoy the process of researching investment opportunities. It's not the sort of profession that you enter without having a passion for understanding the many influences affecting a company or industry.

My years as an analyst and then mutual fund manager at T. Rowe Price taught me lessons that prepared me for the New Normal. First and foremost, it taught me that successful investors stay away from the crowd. They do things their way, make their own decisions, and accept the consequences of their actions. On Wall Street they say, "Don't fight the tape." But that doesn't mean you should be a conformist.

As you have no doubt figured out, I had little preparation for a career specializing in technology companies. In college, I took precisely two engineering courses. But T. Rowe Price needed a technology analyst in the summer of 1982. So when I arrived, that's what they assigned me to do. Remember that in 1982, tech was hardly the prize arena it became in the 1990s. It was more like Death Valley for investors.

Initially, T. Rowe Price asked me to cover two sectors—software and defense electronics. Bad idea. I was trying to learn the business of equity research while covering two industries at once. After about six months, my boss took me aside and gave me a "pep talk," in which he explained that if I didn't get my act together in a hurry, I would be asked to leave. The next day I dropped one of my two coverage areas, focused all my energy on the other, and did much better. This is where I learned about the importance of focus.

Tech stocks struggled through most of the 1980s in a bear market, so I needed to be pretty creative to survive, much less succeed. I worked really hard, experimented a lot, figured out a few things, and just kept at it. When T. Rowe Price started the Science & Technology Fund in 1987, tech was still in a bear market. By then, though, I had figured out that I was better off ignoring the established categories, where IBM and others ruled, and instead focusing all my energy on the emerging personal computer industry. Rather than sitting at my desk and reading reports, I spent all of my time at trade shows and conferences. I believed in my strategy and invested some of my own savings in technology products that my firm wouldn't pay for. I grew to understand how technology products—and technology businesses—work. This is where I learned that working hard is important, but working smart is essential. Like most businesses, the investment business is about results. Unlike most businesses, mutual fund portfolio managers have a scorecard in the newspaper every day.

I learned to pay careful attention to everything from shifts in consumer behavior to stock market structure to new technology to the inability of companies to change in the face of competitive threats. I learned how to trust people. I learned even more about myself. I learned what I was good at and—just as important—what I wasn't good at. I learned to offset my weaknesses by working with others whose skills complemented mine. I also decided to be a team player, volunteering for lots of jobs no one else wanted to do. Over a period of years I learned the ins and outs of running an investment business.

Then I became an entrepreneur. I spent nine wonderful years at T. Rowe Price, developing my skills and working with a fabulous group of people. For the first eight years, I never gave entrepreneurship a moment's thought. But when Microsoft shipped Windows 3.0 in 1990, I sensed that the technology bear market would have to end, and I realized that I was in a unique position to take advantage of the bull market to come. I also realized that mutual funds were not the best structure for my skills. I needed something that would permit me to invest in venture capital, as well as public stocks. No such model existed, so my colleague John Powell and I invented it with our partners from the venture capital firm of Kleiner Perkins Caufield & Byers. It took a year to make Integral Capital Partners happen, but in the process, John and I became entrepreneurs. As I look back, I realize that those days were a lot like now. The economy was emerging from recession. The economic rules were changing and no one was certain how to respond. So John and I decided to take control of our future.

The 1990s turned out to be very exciting. Integral got up and running in 1991, just as the economy and the market started to pick up. We had a great run, but by 1997, it was clear to me that Silicon Valley and Wall Street were both out of control. I didn't know when the cycle would end, but I decided not to wait. I returned to my entrepreneurial mode, looking for ways to navigate the bear market that would surely come. In partnership with my friend Jim Davidson, I planned the Next Big Thing. The result was Silver Lake Partners. Like Integral, Silver Lake turned out to be a good idea at the right time. The fund was structured to buy huge positions in technology market leaders, then help the management team navigate a difficult environment. Silver Lake's long-term, value-added approach would enable it to take advantage of market declines. The bust hit, but Silver Lake sailed on through. At Integral, we also moved boldly, returning half the fund's capital to investors—most of it in cash—in early 2000.

In the first half of 2003, as Silver Lake was planning for its second partnership, I realized that an investment opportunity existed to apply the Silver Lake model to the media and entertainment industry. So I gathered some friends and began working on what would become Elevation Partners.

Like Silver Lake, Elevation Partners is a private equity fund, but it targets the media and entertainment industry. Elevation got started with a phone call from Bono. We got to know each other a few years ago, when Bono was curious about the Grateful Dead's band-to-fan business model. Like the Dead, to whom I was a business adviser, U2 controlled its own intellectual property, and I wound up advising them on a (I can't resist the pun!) pro bono basis. In late 2003, on the advice of his neighbor—who happened to be an investor of mine—Bono called me on my cell to discuss an investment idea he had. I was ready for a new challenge, as was Marc Bodnick, one of my Silver Lake colleagues. We showed the idea to John Riccitiello, the president of Electronic Arts. By coincidence, on that very day Fred Anderson, Apple Computer's finance chief, announced his retirement. John and Fred both joined us, as did a former colleague of Marc's, Bret Pearlman.

That is what I do during the daytime. At night, Ann and I play in a rock 'n' roll band, the Flying Other Brothers. Playing music is something I love, and it has always been a serendipitous asset in my day job. In the youthful days of the PC industry, there were frequent jam sessions at trade shows and conferences. My ability to sing and play a few hundred songs made me an invaluable player in those sessions, and it opened the door to some of the most important people in the industry. It's how I met Microsoft cofounder Paul Allen (guitar), Borland founder Philippe Kahn (saxophone), the top technology people at Apple, and lots of others. Years later, it helped me connect with the Grateful Dead, U2, Pearl Jam, and other bands that were trying to figure out what the Internet meant for them. Those relationships helped me understand the opportunity in media and entertainment, which ultimately led me to Elevation.

My life has been anything but a straight line. It has had tremendous highs and serious lows. The same is true of my career. But every setback has provided a foundation for the next move. Every lesson has helped me improve myself. And now I'm ready for the New Normal.

Enough about me. In the following section, I offer a brief look at how the New Normal has affected the key spheres of our lives. This section will provide context for the New Normal and the rest of the book. Next, I zero in on ten critical insights that are changing our world and delivering a promising future that is already at our doorstep.

GETTING STARTED

The first step toward success in the New Normal is to realign yourself to reality. Each of us has a self-image, but it might need some reevaluation now that we're in the New Normal. Get out a piece of paper and write down the things you believe about yourself. Focus in particular on the notions that apply to family, career, and personal finance. Throughout this book, I will pose questions that will help you assess these beliefs in the context of the reality of the New Normal. This reality check is your first move toward a better future.

Open the door. Take your first step. Enjoy the journey.

Part One

REALITY CHECK

.1.

TECHNOLOGY: IT'S ABOUT YOU

Finally, after decades when most technological innovations were directed at the needs of corporations, the cool stuff is aimed at us. That's right, in the New Normal, consumers are the beneficiary of the most dramatic technological advances. Don't believe me? Just check out the displays wherever computers are sold. When a store wants to show off the best PCs, it doesn't run a business application; it demonstrates consumer products, such as interactive entertainment or video editing. Today, the hottest PC hardware isn't in enterprises, it's in homes. It's not just the world of personal computers that is now ruled by the rest of us. The consumer technology revolution is happening everywhere. And it's just hitting its stride. We live in an era of uncertainty, but here's something on which you can rely: consumer technology will get better and better and better. Now it's *you* who are being empowered, and just as we've seen with businesses, the benefits will go to those who take advantage of emerging technology.

As hard as it may be to believe, businesses are now getting derivative benefits from products designed for consumers. Businesses are also figuring out how to leverage consumer products to improve business processes. Instant Messaging (IM), which started out as a consumer application, has improved the productivity of millions of people in businesses across the country. Soon, automobile insurers will be able to streamline the claims-adjustment process by having customers photograph fender damage from their cell-phone cameras and transmit the evidence in real time.

This shift in the center of gravity of the tech industry began at the dawn of the new millennium. When businesses upgraded their technology in anticipation of Y2K, they replaced every system they had with the latest and greatest. And then came the recession. Corporate buyers of technology basically took three years off. During that hiatus, the technology industry had nothing better to do than cater to the consumer. Remarkably, the downturn in consumer spending that many economists expected never materialized. What happened instead was a flood of compelling new products—DVD players, digital cameras, and iPods—that kept consumers in a spending mode right through the recession. It's not as if every product did great, but enough of them did. Consumer purchases of PCs were nothing special, but demand for flat-panel TVs went bananas.

The combination of rapidly improving price performance and inexpensive manufacturing is delivering a dazzling array of easy-to-use products at prices below the spending limits of the mass market. If you wanted to buy a consumer PC fifteen years ago, the cost was so high that it required you to postpone other major expenditures. At $500 a pop today, PCs are affordable to just about every consumer in America. But the exciting stories relate to products you can carry:

phones, cameras, music players, and the like. These products reflect a valuable lesson that consumers have taught technology companies: products that do one thing really well usually succeed.

In the days when new consumer devices were expensive to produce, vendors tended to load them down with features to justify a high price. The trouble was, on multi-purpose gadgets, many of the functions worked poorly, if at all. Consumers quickly became too savvy to fall for that.

Vendors have gotten smarter, too. When they bring a new product to market, vendors are more often starting with a single-function device. That keeps the price down and increases the probability of a good consumer experience. Take the Roomba, the battery-operated robotic vacuum cleaner that sells for $199 and actually works. You put it in a room and walk away. Roomba does its job—more quietly than traditional vacuum cleaners—and then goes to sleep. If the Roomba had arrived on the scene in the late 1990s, it undoubtedly would have been huge, cost a bundle, and included an FM receiver or CD player aimed at drowning out the vacuum cleaner's noise. Instead, Roomba does just one thing and does it well.

The technology of PCs can easily be repackaged to produce an almost infinite variety of single-purpose products. What's the difference between a PC, a TiVo, and an XBox? The hardware is essentially the same: a microprocessor, a disc drive, lots of memory, and supporting semiconductors. The difference is the software. For PCs, the software is general purpose. For TiVo and the XBox, it is application specific. When you optimize a system for a single application, "ease of use" is no longer an oxymoron. Reliability improves. And the technology can be very inexpensive to manufacture. Consider DVD players. When I started writing this book in late 2003, DVD players had just dropped below the hundred-dollar mark. Five months later you could pick one up for thirty-nine dollars. It's no surprise, but DVD players achieved mass penetration in U.S. households faster than any consumer electronics device in history. I predict we'll see a succession of other products break that record.

There are several reasons why we'll see record-setting penetration of consumer products throughout the New Normal. For one thing, as the world becomes more accustomed to technology, the most compelling innovations move from new to normal very quickly. We've finally ended the era in which consumers must *learn* how to operate a cell phone or personal computer. Downloading images of your newborn from a digital camera to a PC is not as easy as it should be, but easy enough that a remarkable number of people can do it. Today, 78 percent of households with children have a PC. When it comes to consumer technology, the unbelievably costly training period is over.

The other big driver of consumer technology is market opportunity. Businesses already spend half their capital expenditures on technology; they're not going to devote 75 percent. Thanks to Y2K upgrades, the technology inside most corporations does a good job with today's applications. Until a major new wave of applications comes along, spending will more or less track growth in employment. On the consumer side, however, new and cooler applications come along all the time. No matter how fast your processor or how big your disc drive, there always seems to be a new consumer application that requires more. Best of all, there seems to be no end in sight to consumers' spending power for hot new technologies.

Most of the new consumer devices in recent years have provided entertainment or communications. That will continue, particularly with new applications that leverage the Internet and the wireless communications network. But in coming years, you can expect products across a much broader set of applications. There will be huge demand for anything that helps us feel safer and more in control of our lives. Personal security and home health care are obvious opportunities. We all want innovations that give us more power. Technology has already transformed the business world, and it is now doing the same for individuals. As an individual, you can choose to ignore these innovations if you want, but other people are not going to ignore them—and they will benefit. There's no reason why *you* can't, too.

And companies will benefit as well. While they may not be making large investments in traditional hardware and software right now, they are using technology to improve the customer experience and lower costs at the same time. What do I mean? Take a look at the instant success of airport check-in kiosks. You have the choice of waiting in line to receive your boarding pass or swiping a credit card and grabbing your boarding pass as it slides out from a machine in a matter of seconds. Only a few months after they were introduced, those kiosks became incredibly popular—saving money for the airlines, shortening wait times, and making customers happy. Another example: Galp Energia, Portugal's soon-to-be-privatized energy company, operates thirteen hundred gas stations in Portugal and Spain. When it became the first in its industry to offer a thumbprint biometric payment option, the response was overwhelming. Customers—some of whom live in tiny villages where high-tech has made few inroads—raced to pay by thumb. You can't turn back from that sort of progress.

.2.

GOVERNMENT: OUT OF THE DRIVER'S SEAT

Governments are a lot like people. Some of them get it: India, China, and Finland are examples. Some don't, such as Iran, Nigeria, and Indonesia. Some ride high one day, but have a rough time dragging themselves out of bed the next. Japan, for example. As technology and worldwide free markets link the planet and create unprecedented opportunities for growth, the key to a nation's economic success increasingly depends on its leaders' ability to accept the obvious: Globalization is not going away.

Think about it for a moment. Just as there is no benefit to undoing the sprawling and magnificent telecommunications networks that now wrap the Earth, there is no benefit to impeding the river of goods, services, and labor that wants to flow naturally among nations according to the free-market forces of supply and demand. Even if it were not too late to turn back the clock, that would be the wrong answer. Globalization has been a powerful force for good, in the United States and around the world.

The first step toward effective government is a recognition that the role of government has changed. The European Union (EU) is the first example of nations attempting to subsume their identity to gain competitive advantage in a global economy. Finding the political will to give up a national identity is not easy. Nation-states have dominated the political scene for centuries, and nationalism remains a powerful force, even in Europe. Several key countries in Europe have refused to join the EU. And those that have still retain more independence than the EU might like. On the plus side of the equation, globalization has blurred the cultural distinctions among nations, lowering the barriers to partnerships.

One of the big changes during the 1990s was the power shift from national governments to the global free market and to the financial markets. After the fall of the Berlin Wall, globalization propelled the economies of the world to a decade of spectacular growth. Technology and globalization combined to transform the world economy, with huge benefits—in the form of low prices on goods—to consumers in all developed countries.

The economic downturn that began in 2000 exposed the downside of globalization—that lower consumer prices sometimes depend on the migration of commoditized job categories to low-cost labor markets. And it also exposed the limitations faced by governments.

When the Bush administration imposed tariffs on imported steel, the goal was to protect American jobs in the steel industry. What actually happened was quite different. Tariffs increased the cost of steel, which hurt the American industries that depend on it, as well as all the consumers who buy products that include steel. Ultimately, more jobs were lost in automobile manufacturing and other industries than were saved in steel, and the Bush administration eliminated the tariff.

The trouble is, for centuries governments have been accustomed to having a major influence—if not the final say—on a wide range of economic and social issues. The rise of globalization has changed that. In the New Normal, a government that imposes protectionist measures will only succeed in weakening its nation's economy. A government can try to protect jobs. It can try to break up economic monopolies. It can try to enforce environmental regulations beyond its own borders. It can try to manipulate its currency. But it can't do any of these things nearly as effectively as was possible fifteen years ago.

In the New Normal, the strongest nations will be those in which the government is first and best at understanding the evolution of the global economy—and have the flexibility to promote change. One mantra is Globalization rules. Another is Industries come and go, so always make new ones. Trying to protect a particular industry from global competition is a loser's game. "Job protection" is an economic policy that favors the few over the population as a whole. When practiced on a broad scale—as it has been in parts of Western Europe—the effect is to limit economic growth. Countries that protect jobs wind up restraining the economic engine that is entrepreneurship. That sucking sound you hear is entrepreneurs leaving to start companies somewhere else.

The key to job growth is entrepreneurship. In the United States, small businesses create more than two out of every three new jobs and generate more than half of the nation's economic output. Among established economic powers, the United States has the best track record of promoting entrepreneurship.

Throughout the coming decade, forward-looking governments will use policy to increase economic opportunity. It's what Finland did by providing a free and equal education system for all its citizens, from first grade through PhD level (even providing university students with a monthly allowance). Finland's average skill and education level is the highest in Europe. Or look at India. In 1991, when the Indian economy was on the verge of collapse because of overwhelming debt, the then finance minister Dr. Manmohan Singh and Prime Minister P. V. Narasimha Rao, decided to open up the Indian economy and begin privatization of the giant public enterprises. Over the last decade, these policies have resulted in a great degree of liberalization, economic growth, and foreign investment. The reforms haven't been perfect, but India's GDP now is growing at an annual rate of 6 percent.

Then there's the North American Free Trade Agreement. NAFTA reduced the trade barriers between the United States, Canada, and Mexico. NAFTA holds vast promise for improving its participants' economies, and the early results are good. Mexico's economy has made significant gains, improving the stability and security of the region. It is quite possible that future generations may look back on NAFTA as one of the most important economic policies of the twentieth century.

One of the great challenges in the New Normal involves the natural fallout that results from the changing role of government. As governments become less effective, frustration builds in the citizenry. In the United States, this frustration manifests itself not only in polarization of the electorate, but also in a greater stridency. Liberals and conservatives seem to be losing the ability to engage in constructive debate. Instead, we have increasingly nasty arguments about issues large and small. Statesmanship and conciliation have been replaced by partisan attack. What used to be middle ground is now just a black hole.

As with so much in the New Normal, the current political climate may be nothing more than an undesirable side effect of rapid change. The political tone might become more conciliatory as the economy improves. I sure hope it does.

When the global economy rose from the ashes of the Berlin Wall, it established a new style of conflict. Where the Cold War revolved around a massive staring contest between two super powers, the global economy produces continuous small battles among nations of all sizes. Established economic powers are accustomed to getting what they want. Emerging countries want a better deal and now have a bit of leverage with which to get it. We live in an environment of interdependency. The giants are still more powerful than small countries, but they can no longer dictate the terms of economic interaction. Smaller countries have an ability to influence their larger counterparts—and the New Normal—in ways that were impossible during the Cold War. The risk of trade wars is higher than at any time in seventy years.

Meanwhile, the New Normal will give governments greater opportunity to improve the delivery of essential services to their citizens. Here, again, technology is a key enabler. Travel around the planet and you can see the new world unfolding before your eyes. In England, you can watch Web casts of Parliamentary debates. In Australia, you can register your new business online; a process that previously took fifteen days now takes as little as fifteen seconds. In Finland, you can pay your taxes via mobile phone. In Canada, the government-sponsored Job Bank lists opportunities from coast to coast. At peak times, the site gets eighteen thousand hits per minute.

It's starting to happen in the United States as well. The Federal Communications Commission made it astonishingly easy to sign up online for the national do-not-call list. It was so simple that in thirty-one days, from July 1 to August 1, 2003, nearly one-eighth of the households in the entire country were able to register a phone number to opt out of telemarketing calls. That's government doing its job in the New Normal.

.3.

BUSINESS: THE COURAGE TO ACT

The world of business is emerging from a monster hangover, the kind that can be cured only by time and rest.

The mania of the late 1990s persuaded businesses—as well as governments and people in general—of the existence of a New Economy, complete with its own set of rules. Remember the New Economy? The business world temporarily rejected sound principles that had governed it for nearly a century in favor of a make-it-up-as-you-go-along strategy. Even the largest companies drank the Kool-Aid of the New Economy. But the biggest impact occurred in the world of start-ups, where an entire generation of entrepreneurs committed themselves to business plans that had only the smallest chance of success. Today, many of them wish they had been committed, period.

For business, the most obvious manifestation of the New

Normal is a return to traditional metrics: revenues, profits, and cash flow. After five years when companies could simply invent operating metrics—"eyeballs," page views, and the like—businesses are being held accountable for old-fashioned results. It is painful for some, but progress for all. It will put us on firmer footing.

While the New Economy turned out to be an illusion, its consequences were as real as an earthquake, and we are still living with the wreckage. The economy continues to struggle with excess capacity produced by six years of over-the-top capital spending. Executives resize and restructure their businesses without a clear picture of the true level of business activity. Investors continue to harbor unrealistic expectations.

Time and rest have done their best. Now it's time to move on—and to make the most of the post-post-mania environment. And there's a lot of opportunity out there. But here's a glitch: because no one is quite certain what to expect, people are sticking to what has worked most recently for them. During the downturn, companies got accustomed to cutting their capital expenditures, particularly their technology capital expenditures. In a lousy economy, cost cutting is very effective. The longer the downturn, the bigger the payoff from cost cuts. If the downturn lasts long enough, and the recent one certainly did, companies can even get away with not investing in their future. All they have to do is tell their investors that the environment remains uncertain . . . and hope their competitors don't invest.

The recent environment created a challenge for business. Still smarting from the downturn, CEOs wanted to delay capital spending and expense growth as long as they could. They could clearly see that the economy had passed bottom but were reluctant to abandon the cost-cutting policies that worked during the downturn. The perceived risk of making the wrong decision was greater than the perceived risk of doing nothing.

Compounding the situation: businesses are still adapting to the flurry of regulatory reform in securities and corporate governance. Securities and governance regulations play an important role in protecting society from the tendency of both individuals and organizations to operate in their own short-term self-interest. But reform always has unintended consequences. Don't get me wrong. I think the intent of the Sarbanes-Oxley Act of 2002 is very sound. The law, which is aimed at increasing the independence of boards of directors, would work better if it did not impose arbitrarily expensive rules on all companies irrespective of size, but these imperfections can and should be addressed. And Eliot Spitzer is one of my heroes. I think he's doing a great job of restoring some integrity to securities-law enforcement, and he may actually prompt the SEC to start doing the job for which it was created. But there is an unintended consequence of all this reform: it gives managements and boards of directors a built-in excuse to avoid creative and aggressive decision-making. The reflexive response to the new regulations is to do nothing. Directors don't want to do anything that increases their liability.

After the nonsense of the late 1990s, you might question whether the words *creative* and *aggressive* should be used in the same paragraph as the word *corporation.* The important thing is to give people freedom. Freedom for management to do what it thinks is best for the company, shareholders, and employees. Freedom for shareholders to know what is really going on, to have a voice, and to sell shares if they don't like what they see. Freedom for customers to get the best products at the best prices.

Fortunately, the current corporate holding pattern won't last forever. We've got history on our side. Typically, cycles of outrageous behavior are followed by waves of regulation that moderate behavior. When mania turns to bust, it takes a long time for people to get over the consequences—and even longer for them to get courageous again. In general, uncertainty and regulatory reform sustain conservative behavior longer than is good for our economy. At some point, however, a management team always gets bold. It invests in its business. The investment pays off. Competitors are forced to respond. Then other companies read about it and follow suit. Businesses start cranking again. That is the beauty of free markets.

In the New Normal, there are astonishing business opportunities, but they typically don't look like yesterday's opportunities. Neither big businesses nor IPOs will get all the glory. Today, size matters less than at any time in the past fifty years. Thanks to technology, even small businesses can have a global footprint if they leverage the Internet and available tools that are dropping in price even as capabilities increase. Large companies still have lots of opportunity. They can win when it comes to mass customization and mass distribution. But in many parts of the economy, where customization is more important than mass, smaller companies and individuals have a shot at success simply because they can be more focused. It's hard for any company to be good at a hundred different domains at the same time. It's easy for a hundred small companies to be good at one domain each.

Flexibility has replaced scale as the key ingredient for corporate success in uncertain times. All else being equal, most companies would rather be large than small, but nearly everyone has come to appreciate the benefits of flexibility. Since the Internet bust, corporations have been focused on making do with fewer people. They are struggling to develop the ability to grow or shrink according to market conditions. This seismic shift opens up enormous opportunities for start-ups to serve the needs of large companies—to deliver key business processes that enable large companies to respond to the market without having extra employees during lean times. With productivity and flexibility as the most sought-after capabilities, companies will continue to outsource key business processes to third parties, specialist firms that will come in every conceivable size and structure. This is a monster opportunity pounding on the door.

Sure, large companies still have huge advantages, but those advantages have value only in combination with a good business model. As the playing field becomes more level, business models grow in importance. There's simply no room in the economy for companies without a solid one.

To see the importance of business models, consider the examples of Hewlett-Packard and Dell. In 2002, H-P acquired Compaq to create the world's largest vendor of PCs, printers, and other important technology products. The merged company remained the number one vendor of PCs for roughly one fiscal quarter. It couldn't hold that position because its business model, which depends on a hybrid of retail and direct-sales channels, could not keep pace with Dell's. To sell through dealer channels, H-P must bear the enormous expense of building products months in advance, whereas Dell builds most of its products in response to customer orders. Dell's cost savings completely offset H-P's temporary scale advantage. It took Dell only a matter of months to regain the number one position.

Companies with winning business models will sail confidently into the New Normal. Google, which puts unobtrusive, relevant ads in front of people while they search the Web, charges advertisers only for ads that generate sales leads. Pay-for-performance advertising is the hottest thing on Madison Avenue, and it started on the Web.

Lots of business models that worked really well in the 1990s need a facelift for the New Normal. Successful companies will adapt their business model to the times. In an environment where PC industry revenues are growing painfully slowly, Microsoft needs to be creative to sustain its growth. The subscription business model is an answer. Microsoft now encourages customers to view software as a subscription purchase. Increasing numbers of customers have made Microsoft software a line item in their annual budget.

Another example is EMC, the Massachusetts-based leader in storage management systems, which saw its revenue collapse during the bust. EMC was quick to realize that the game was up. It could no longer prosper selling huge arrays of very expensive disk drives. Embracing the inevitable, EMC changed its business model. It cut prices dramatically on storage systems and started buying enterprise software products that could be sold to its high-end customer base. The company now sells a wide range of enterprise software to complement its storage solutions. It is too early to know if the acquisitions will pan out, but win, lose, or draw, EMC is better off. EMC understood that the risk of dramatic change was actually quite acceptable in comparison to the inevitable disaster that would have come from standing still. The company bought itself some time, and with time comes opportunity.

EMC is one of a handful of companies that have taken bold action in the early days of the New Normal. Apple Computer is another. Apple has made a big bet on consumer electronics, a bet that is paying off so far. Again, it's no guarantee of future success, but that's not the point. The world has changed, and Apple has changed with it.

There are countless companies facing questions similar to those faced by EMC and Apple. Among them are Lucent, a leading vendor of technology for voice and data communications, and Sun Microsystems, the leading vendor of computer systems based on the Unix operating system. Both Lucent and Sun were high fliers in the 1990s. Both have come upon hard times. Lucent has been all but forced to take aggressive action. Thanks to a huge cash reserve, Sun does not feel the same sense of urgency. As a result, Sun is still trying to decide if aggressive action is called for and, if so, what form it should take. Meanwhile, such vendors as Dell and IBM are taking market share from Sun. Industry analysts and pundits have been quick to write off Lucent and Sun, but the final chapter on these companies has not been written. I hope they move aggressively to reinvent themselves. But time is of the essence. Business models cannot remain under construction for long.

Just as corporations will be increasingly dependent on strong business models, they'll also need to be more thoughtful in how they use technology. The encouraging news for large enterprises is that start-ups are no longer a threat in most industries. Freed from the pressure to deploy flaky Internet technology to impress investors who were dazzled by start-ups, large companies now can concentrate on using really good Internet technology to gain sustainable competitive advantage.

For corporations, making the most of technology in the New Normal means taking a decentralized approach. Technology is no longer so mysterious that it requires a priesthood of IT professionals to make all the decisions. Instead, enterprises in every sector of the economy simply need to understand how technology affects their particular business and what they can do to take advantage of it. This requires effort at all levels of the organization. Top management needs to be involved in technology strategy, and the whole company needs to take responsibility for making it work. Management needs to delegate more and more of the specification and deployment responsibility to the operating folks who will actually use the stuff. This will give IT a new and more valuable role: partnering with operating people to make the business work better. When this happens, technology becomes more like other mature categories of capital expenditure, such as forklifts and office furniture, and it drives value creation.

Meanwhile, another new trend will continue in the New Normal: cycle times are shrinking. The trip from start-up to success is faster than ever. The same goes for the trip from success to failure.

One of the biggest lessons of the 1990s is that it's in everyone's interest to identify success or failure as quickly as possible. Customers and investors are less patient than ever. As you can imagine, there is both good and bad in this. On the one hand, it creates tremendous pressure to deliver positive results quickly. On the other hand, there are new market opportunities—including the market for tools and services to help businesses understand faster than they could before what works and what doesn't.

So the New Normal combines a return to traditional business metrics—sales, profits, and cash flow—with new rules. The early lessons are clear: technology enables businesses to prosper with fewer employees. Flexibility is key to prospering in uncertain times. And globalization creates opportunities for small companies, as well as large ones.

As always, delay is still a strategy. But it's a really, really bad one.

.4.

MEDIA: DIGITAL CHANGES EVERYTHING

Technology has had an impact on every sector of the economy, but no industry has been transformed more than that of media and entertainment. The transition from analog to digital improved the quality of entertainment, while also making it cheaper to produce and distribute. Thanks to technology, the cost of players for CDs, DVDs, and video games has collapsed, radically altering the way we consume media. Where media was once confined to cinemas and living rooms, it is now pervasive. Battery-operated devices the size of a pack of playing cards can hold an entire music library. New cars can have built-in video and DVD in the back seat. Jet Blue and Lufthansa offer air passengers satellite television at their seats.

The technology that has made media and entertainment content available at lower prices and in new places has had two dramatic effects. First, it has lowered the unit cost of media and entertainment content by reducing the distribution cost. Second, by making media available in new places, technology has effectively increased the time we have available to be entertained. This comes at a time when people in developed nations have more money to spend on media and entertainment. The key driver of media and entertainment spending is disposable income, which has risen dramatically over the past twenty-five years. On top of all this, globalization has grown the market by creating a middle class with disposable income in countries such as China and India. The combination of more disposable income, lower unit costs, more time, and new markets is a perfect storm of good news for the media and entertainment industry.

To date, consumers have gotten more benefit from the good news than has the industry. It used to be that media and entertainment companies controlled consumer access to content, which allowed them to maintain high prices. But technology and the Internet have undercut the industry's stranglehold on distribution. As consumers, we have more media and entertainment options than ever. We can watch a television show on a network or use TiVo to watch it later. Or we can watch a past episode of that show in syndication on a cable channel. Or buy past episodes on DVD. For owners of content, this proliferation of distribution channels represents an economic opportunity, but for owners of distribution—broadcast television networks or cable systems, for example—it poses a serious threat. Broadcast networks are losing advertising dollars due to diminished audiences. Cable systems have gained share relative to broadcast networks, but are threatened by alternatives such as DVD and video games. A similar thing happened to the major music labels. They were slow to respond to the Internet and eventually faced a major change in the competitive environment. Instead of competing against other labels, the major labels found themselves in competition with digital copies of their own songs being distributed free by consumers.

In the United States, we consume more media—television, music, movies, and books—than any other country. We produce more media than any other country. Brace yourself. Changes are happening at warp speed. Everything about media—from who owns it to how it's produced to whether it can or should be controlled, and if so, how—is in a disorienting state of flux. Music companies have struggled with piracy for five years. The movie industry will soon struggle to protect its movies from being copied as high-speed Internet access makes them more accessible. Computer makers are battling television manufacturers over the flat-screen television business. Cable television companies are muscling into phone company territory—using Internet technology to deliver voice calls over cable.

I suspect nobody knows how it will all play out. But there are some important currents to understand.

First: The most important media producer is you.

Imagine the next time a government tries to suppress an important news event. They won't stand a chance. Witnesses will whip out a cell phone, take a picture or video and put it up on the Web. Instant journalism. That's what embedded cameras and video recorders in cell phones will deliver. It's an astonishing blow to anyone attempting to obstruct freedom.

Throughout the New Normal, digital media's reach and impact will radically expand. Some will be bewildered by the change. Others will revel in it. And our culture will intensify its struggle to adjust. The tug of war between the First Amendment right to free speech and the Fourth Amendment right to privacy will come to a head, keeping our courts occupied and coloring our world the way the civil rights struggle colored it a generation ago.

Second: Media is everywhere.

From where you sit, it may appear that everything about the media world is getting worse. Quantity of media seems to be overwhelming quality. New forms of unwanted information are streaming into your life. Some of it good. Much of it bad. But all of it available for the choosing. The institutions that "protected" you in the past—the ones that decided what kinds of media were suitable—won't come to your rescue. But they also won't be able to tell you what you can read, watch, or hear.

You have freedom of choice as never before. That just means you've got to take more responsibility, by making yourself far more conscious of the flow of material that finds its way into your life and by taking advantage of the new filtering technology that is becoming available in tandem with digital media. TiVo does a great job of helping you maintain control of television content. Common Sense Media helps parents decide what media content is appropriate for their children and how to talk to them about whatever content they are exposed to. In the New Normal, we'll see a flourishing market of products designed to let you take charge of your world. This is a huge business opportunity for both large and small companies.

There are other things to worry about and other solutions. Media organizations, now required to feed the endless appetites of their twenty-four-hours-a-day monsters, have redefined what constitutes "news." It's far easier and considerably less expensive for media operators to package opinion and analysis than to produce solidly reported news. Increasingly, viewers are confusing the former with the latter. This is a scary trend that requires consumers of news to be far more aware and discerning about what they hear—and what they think they know. The growing shortage of unbiased information puts the burden on people to seek out objectivity if they want to be well informed. Accurate news reporting is out there, but you have to put some effort into finding it.

Meanwhile, ease of entry has caused a rapid fragmentation of a media universe that once seemed easy to grasp. Like paramecia dividing, the number of media outlets has grown exponentially. This diffusion of media allows each outlet—cable channels, Web sites, and the rest—to bear a specialized identity and point of view. The natural inclination is to rush to those that affirm our existing beliefs, while ignoring those espousing different viewpoints.

This is where digital media in the New Normal can become a trap. Unprecedented access to limitless information can paradoxically enable us to limit our media to outlets that reinforce our existing beliefs. As a culture, we risk moving farther and farther from any hope of meeting at a common middle ground. Again, that challenge creates the need for personal responsibility. But the benefits of personal responsibility are huge. If you understand what is really going on—not just what some "expert" tells you—you will be positioned to prosper in the New Normal.

Digital technology has radically altered the economics of media production and distribution. The cost of making music CDs now runs about a buck apiece, well within the budget of most garage bands. The cost of publishing one's own "newspaper" as a Web site is astonishingly low. As a result, there are countless Web sites and Web logs (blogs) where people share their view of events. Even a sixth-grader now is capable of making and distributing a film. What happens when everybody can become a music producer, journalist, or film director? An eruption of creativity. That's the bright side.

At the same time, everybody can become a media bootlegger. Media piracy will continue to flourish in the New Normal. Technology enables both legitimate creators of media and media pirates. We can expect a constant battle between them. Neither side is likely to sustain an advantage for long.

This is the great irony of media in the New Normal. Each major advance brings us unimaginable access to information. But it also increases the challenge of learning how to adjust. And we're far from being well adjusted.

.5.

CAREERS: NEVER AN IDLE MOMENT

For the most part, the fifty years between World War II and the Internet mania were a laid-back period where you didn't have to worry about your career. Sure, you had to decide on a career itself, plot your path to advancement, and yes, you had to work hard. But for the most part, once you took a job with your company, your union, or your government, you started down a track that you could not easily get off. You did your job. You put in your time. You washed your car on the weekend. You had relatively little control, but benefited from the substantial safety net provided by your paternalistic employer. This may have been the career environment of your father and grandfather.

Then somebody added a psychedelic drug to the Kool-Aid. The late 1990s brought with them a gold rush that lured perfectly sane people to take risks that would have been unimaginable only a few years earlier. Career opportunity was a field of gems. You picked one up, turned it over, and if it wasn't the diamond of your dreams you put it back and went on to the next gem. Once you picked your jewel, you endured unimaginably long work hours in a job you couldn't explain with coworkers you couldn't stand just for a shot at walking away rich in eighteen months. You couldn't imagine not being able to retire in a few short fiscal quarters.

Well, the downturn that followed the Internet mania retired *you* from that way of life. And suddenly, you landed—*splat!*—in the New Normal. Whether it took you days, weeks, or months to realize it, your world no longer was conducive to the taking of uncalculated risks and the winning of instant fortunes. Perhaps it never was. But here's what was truly unnerving: it also wasn't possible to return to the stability of an earlier era. Even if you had a job in the most stable of companies, your world suddenly bore no resemblance to the calm and predictability of the pre–Internet mania. The only thing you could predict with relative certainty was that there no longer *was* any certainty.

Unlike the premania period, corporations are now better able to leverage technology to create lean, ultraefficient operations that require as few humans as possible. Unlike the premania period, corporate managements—reeling from an economic downturn and pressured to boost productivity—refuse to risk their fate by doing anything as daring as increasing headcount. These behaviors still linger, even as the economy improves.

The question is: Now what?

The challenge of the New Normal is perception. The world is different and we all must change how we look at it. It's a time when there are few, if any, safety nets. It's a time when you'll need to take more responsibility for your own future. In all other respects, though, the New Normal is a time of great prospects—you just have to get past the uncertainty. The global free market offers a wide range of new career opportunities. Really. The challenge is to pick the one that is right for you. Free from the illusion of instant riches, you'll have the luxury of being more thoughtful about what it is you like doing and the kind of people you like to work with. So please follow my lead and embrace the inevitable. Embrace change and uncertainty. If you want to move forward, you really don't have much of a choice.

There are a few fundamental rules for careers in the New Normal.

First, if you want to be successful in the New Normal, cultivate skills that are too valuable for outsourcing. Or become the person to whom businesses outsource.

Accept the reality that every company is looking at its business processes to see which are core competencies and which can be outsourced. Job classifications will be outsourced throughout the economy. Companies may be willing to pay more per hour to an outsourcer to avoid the high cost of benefits and the operational inflexibility associated with hiring an employee. Outsourcing has been going on for decades. The only change is that more industries are affected. Like the software industry. Years ago, it was something of an art form to develop software for mainframe and client-server environments. Now it is a commodity and outsourcing some of the jobs overseas makes economic sense. Obviously, that's very painful in the short term for the people who lose their jobs, but it's the right answer for the economy as a whole.

Are there safe jobs? A few, but "safe" is not an adjective that should modify the word "jobs" in the New Normal. Doctors and nurses do work that is hard to outsource. There is a trend toward outsourcing the review of X-ray, CT, and MRI images, but most medical functions must be performed where the patients are. Developing software for customized business processes or filming industrial videos or managing investments are all high-value jobs in which it helps to be located near your customer or supplier. In reality, there are "safe" jobs in every industry. But a job classification that is safe at one business may be ripe for outsourcing at another.

Corporations will have a massive need for independent contractors or small businesses that can deliver products or services that help them address shifts in market demand. As much as companies fear growth in headcount, they must find a way to meet demand for whatever it is they sell. This raises incredible opportunities for outsourcers—either big firms or independent contractors—to pick up the slack, typically at higher rates of pay.

The tool sets available today, especially the current state of telecommunications, allow virtually anybody to set up an independent operation and perform work for companies around the world without leaving their computer. Meanwhile, the Internet gives entrepreneurs access to an endless supply of information to help them prepare—to study possible markets and identify potential clients. That's right, the same advances that are putting so many people out of work can be used to help entrepreneurs make the most of the New Normal.

Second, get comfortable with uncertainty. To do so, you must first accept the fact that uncertainty is not going away.

Third, to succeed in the New Normal you will have to become more aware of your environment. You need to be conscious of opportunities, aggressive about developing your own flexible network of support, and skilled at managing time and multiple projects. You will need to be capable of developing new and valuable skills. Never stop doing these things. Do these things and the New Normal will deliver far more prospects and prosperity than either the postwar years or the mania.

These activities will serve you well not only in your current career, but also in your second, third, and possibly fourth careers.

That's the other major change in the New Normal. Based on a combination of factors, it is more than likely that you will have not one career but a succession of different careers. For one thing, the economy will keep changing. For another, people are living longer. That might mean you have to delay retirement in order to support your parents. With Social Security and Medicare far from assured, it might mean that you have to delay retirement in order to support yourself.

Here again, the rewards go to those who are most flexible and willing to adapt to change. The winners will be people who view the trend toward successive careers not as a negative but as a chance to try new things. Solid planning, too, will become critical to success in subsequent careers. There is no doubt that you will have the opportunity to get very good at planning. You'll have more of it to do.

.6.

FINANCE: EVERYBODY'S A PROFESSIONAL INVESTOR

As someone who has devoted the past twenty-two years of his life to investing and who has painfully studied and adapted to every Wall Street undulation, I can say with confidence that conditions have never been more advantageous for individuals to be successful in the stock market.

Don't get me wrong. Investors who watched their net worth plummet during the Internet bust have reason to be soured on Wall Street. Observers of the mutual funds scandal have reason to be distrustful. There has been too much shameful behavior on Wall Street. And, yes, the stock market has become unpredictable, with off-and-on elements of the same kind of manic behavior we saw in the late 1990s. It's understandable that individual investors would react to all of this with cynicism and fear. It's really hard to see the upside.

Okay, here it is. Individuals have more advantages on Wall Street than ever before, at a time when those advantages are really valuable. I go into this in great detail in the chapter entitled "New Rules for Winning on Wall Street's Level Field," but let me give you an inkling of what is to come. Largely as a result of recent regulations and technology advances, individuals can compete successfully with institutional investors. Individuals now have access to virtually the same information as professional investors. Unfortunately, it's happening at a time when individual investors are a bit shell-shocked—still trying to recover from Internet mania losses and still waiting for another boom.

The regulatory changes might not have been the best thing for valuations and research, but they've certainly evened up the game. The Security and Exchange Commission's Regulation Fair Disclosure (Reg. FD), adopted in 2000, requires that whenever a public company releases any information, it must be made available to the general public at the same time as institutional investors and analysts. One unintended consequence of Reg. FD is that companies choose to be less open with institutional investors than in the past. Because institutions—mutual funds and the like—dominate the market, the effect of less openness is more uncertainty, which translates into lower valuations. Meanwhile, large investment banks are no longer allowed to have their research analysts and bankers talk to each other, which has reduced the quality of research.

The market's decline and the associated reduction in trading volume have also reduced the quantity of Wall Street research. At last count, 44 percent of all Nasdaq companies have no research coverage at all. Another 14 percent had only one analyst. With so little research coverage, information inefficiencies are increasingly commonplace.

But if you're willing to learn the right questions to ask and to make the time to do your own research, these changes can work in your favor. The data's available and you have the tools—namely, the Internet—to get at it. If you limit your investing to industry sectors you understand, and if you use common sense, you can compete very effectively with the pros.

It might seem daunting to take on more responsibility. Being empowered is as scary as not being empowered was before. Trust me, though. Being empowered is better.

Despite the new environment, most of Wall Street continues to invest just as it did before the market collapse. In stocks, investors still seem to favor momentum over value. It amazes me that so many investors continue to focus on hypergrowth stories, given the more favorable tax treatment of dividends.

In the New Normal, the most attractive risk-reward will be in investments with two ways to win. By that I mean investments with a solid core business that can provide a reasonable rate of return, but also a growth opportunity that can turbocharge your returns. For example, imagine a mature company that is a market leader in its business but has an exciting growth opportunity. If the valuation is low enough that you can get a reasonable return just from the core business—and if you get the growth opportunity for "free"—then the stock is a winner. In the current market environment, there are more stocks like this than you might realize. But they might not be the names recommended by your broker.

.7.

EDUCATION: IT NEVER ENDS

In the New Normal, the double whammy of rapid change and longer life expectancy has created an incentive for all of us to learn new things and develop new skills. If we are likely to have multiple careers, it makes sense to get prepared. Getting prepared is straightforward . . . if you are open to it.

While it may make sense for some people to go back to school, that won't be a viable option for most of us. Work and kids and all the other things going on in our lives force us to be creative about learning. No problem. Half the battle is knowing that you need to keep expanding your horizons.

In the New Normal, detailed knowledge of any business subject—domain expertise—is a great starting point. You are probably already a domain expert at whatever you do professionally today. But that domain expertise may not carry you as far as you want to go. The good news is that a world that is changing constantly produces innumerable opportunities to develop domain expertise. There are always new domains. Somebody has to be the expert. Choose wisely and you may put yourself on a new and better career track. Either way, domain expertise will make you a more desirable employee or contractor.

More than at any time in the past, there is huge upside to being open to opportunities that increase your knowledge. Like so many other areas of the New Normal, your ability to succeed is inextricably linked with your willingness to assume personal responsibility. Volunteer for new projects. Many new projects turn out to be dead ends, but all big opportunities start out as new projects somewhere.

If your employer doesn't offer much in the way of intellectual stimulation, just go to the Internet. Creative opportunities for continuing education are surfacing to meet the rising demand. Check out the Web site for Massachusetts Institute of Technology (www.mit.edu), then follow the links to OpenCourseWare. MIT has given the universe a priceless gift: free education. One of the world's top educational institutions, MIT is posting all two thousand of its courses on the Internet, everything from course notes and tests to reading lists and video lectures. At last count, more than seven hundred courses were already available to anyone with a browser. No, you receive neither credit nor a degree from MIT, but, as students from hundreds of countries around the world have discovered, you will learn material that can be incredibly beneficial.

To address the challenge of studying alone, there's even an opportunity to link to learning communities where others are taking the courses. It's not available for every course, but it is for such popular ones as Introduction to Computers and Engineering Problem Solving, Real Estate Finance and Investment, and Intermediate Applied Microeconomics. By linking to others taking the courses, individuals can collaborate, form study groups, and get the support that will help them learn.

There's more free education, if you look for it. Managing the Digital Enterprise is an online course offered by Professor Michael Rappa of North Carolina State University. Created in 1998 to be used in conjunction with a graduate course he teaches at North Carolina State University, it is made available to the public as a free resource that can be adopted by other instructors to teach courses of their own. Immensely popular, one major consulting firm has made the course a requirement for thousands of its employees.

If you are wondering where to steer your children's education, I would recommend that you encourage them to focus on communications skills and foreign languages. Communications skills are critical, but the sad reality of secondary education in the United States is that far too many children graduate from high school without learning how to write and speak well. When it comes to languages, focus on the big populations. Spanish is taught widely, but I suspect Mandarin Chinese will be more valuable over the next two decades.

A final word: for many people, it's a struggle just to get work and home life accomplished each day, and the thought of taking even an online course seems unrealistic. There are books on many practical topics and Internet services that can bring you specific information in areas you think would be useful to you. If you are wondering where the time will come from, just remember that you are your first priority. Investing in yourself might be difficult, but it will be well worth it.

.8.

FAMILY: THE INSTITUTION YOU CAN SAVE

Amid the uncertainty and fear of the New Normal, the difference between success and failure might rest on having a solid support system to keep you going when venerable institutions such as church, employer, and government fall short of expectations. No institution matters more today than family. Face it. Most other institutions have become unreliable. You can't count on your government to take care of your needs over the long haul or your employer to ensure your continued economic well-being. Religion may be a source of solace and inspiration, but for many, the scandals and turmoil of recent years have added an element of stress to what used to be an oasis of peace. The breakdown of institutions over the past thirty years has been a gradual process, the effects of which were masked as we enjoyed the benefits of the long economic expansion that began in 1945.

Many people include the family in the roll call of dying institutions. There is little doubt that the nuclear family has taken huge hits over the past thirty years. The 2000 U.S. census found that nuclear families consisting of a father, mother, and kids make up less than 25 percent of U.S. households. That figure, the lowest ever recorded, includes "blended" families, in which one of the spouses brings in children from a previous marriage. In fact, more U.S. households contain a single person (26 percent) than traditional nuclear families. But our society has redefined the model to include a variety of family types—everything from single-parent families, which are very common, to the not-so-common "share" families, in which noncohabitating, nonintimate male-female couples partner to bear and raise their own biological children. The institution of family, in whatever form, remains a positive force in the lives of most people. Best of all, the family, more than any other institution, is one over which you can expect to have some sway.

Family has always been important as a stabilizing influence, but today family plays that role in new and different ways. In the Old Normal, when life was more predictable, career, religion, and family were areas where people made choices early in life and barely gave them a second thought. Conformity was king. If you had trouble in your family, you went to great pains to cover it up. If life at home got you down, you may have had the option of retreating into a career where there was a high degree of steadiness and where you got your daily doses of motivation, fun, reassurance, and comradeship. No longer.

In the New Normal, careers can provide great satisfaction and monetary reward, but they are unlikely to provide much stability and comfort. Sure, you might get stability and comfort from time to time, but you definitely shouldn't count on it. With jobs demanding more time and creating more stress, making home life a steadying force in your life should be a priority.

Like everything else about the New Normal, the mission of strengthening family ties will require a conscious effort. And like everything else, the tools are there to help. Technology will enable a new generation of work-at-home careers. Even if your job requires you to show up at an office, technology makes it possible to stay close to everyone who is important to you. Communication solidifies families and it has never been easier to stay in constant touch.

Increasingly, technology is coming to the rescue of families. You don't have to worry about forgetting your niece's birthday or an anniversary because you can get reminders from your PDA or from an online retailer eager to make you look like a hero. Being thoughtful takes less effort than ever: you can send roses or a new best seller with a single click. BlackBerry. Pagers. You might dismiss these devices as being unnecessary for your job. But that's not the point. If they help you stay close to your family, they're indispensable.

I believe the benefits of a stable family are greater than at any time in memory, but you have to be willing to work at it. In a world where careers demand more time, when kids lives are scheduled as never before, and where there are fewer support systems available to share the burden, it's really hard for parents to keep everything in balance. Extended family is often far-flung, and friends come and go as their careers necessitate moves.

If my most important word of advice is to use technology to stay in touch with your family, the second most important is to get involved in your family's technology strategy. Technology is a huge force in family life—whether you like it or not—so you might as well get with the program. All that is required is a little common sense. A word of caution: It's fine to let your teenager install new software on the family PC. But if you delegate your family's information technology (IT) strategy to a teenager, the results are likely to disappoint you.

Technology is an enormously powerful tool in the home, but it requires some care. For example, there is no teacher built into the Internet to ensure that children develop good academic habits. As a consequence, there's an enormous payoff for parents who spend time with their kids as they learn to surf the Web. Parents are the best teachers when it comes to instructing children about academic honesty when they do research. Parents can also prepare their children for dealing with the pitfalls of the Web, whether in chat rooms or Web sites with inappropriate material. On the other side of the equation, parents can help children develop their thirst for knowledge. Anything that strikes their interest can be learned about more easily and instantly than ever before through the Internet.

By taking advantage of available technology, you can overcome one of the biggest obstacles to strong families: the scarcity of time spent together. Technology itself provides the activity for time with children—playing video games, helping with online homework, or seeking an answer for a curious mind. But technology can also increase the amount of time you spend as a family. The act of paying bills online takes a fraction of the time required to sit down and write out checks. Shopping online saves hours. E-mail and now shared calendaring shaves valuable time off coordinating any activity from a school event to Little League to a family reunion. In the New Normal, family time management can be made easier, if you work at getting the systems in place to optimize technology. In the scheme of things, what's more valuable than time spent with your family?

And in the New Normal, you should feel free to use the word *family* in the broadest sense. Blood relatives? Friends? Neighbors? The guidelines regarding what constitutes a family will continue to evolve throughout the New Normal. Ann and I don't have children, but we have what we call a thermonuclear family, which includes the band, my Elevation business partners, and our godchildren, Jack, Kate, and Meg. We buy a lot of presents at birthdays and the holidays, but our life is richer for it.

It's your family. You get to define it on your own terms. Just give it the importance it deserves.

Part Two

A ROAD MAP THROUGH THE NEW NORMAL

.9.

INDIVIDUALS ARE MORE IMPORTANT THAN EVER

What do J. K. Rowling, Dr. Robert Atkins, and Steve Jobs have in common?

They're all individuals who have changed the world. All by themselves, they have changed the way we live. J. K. Rowling has single-handedly persuaded a generation of kids that reading a seven-hundred-page book is a totally normal endeavor, expanding their vocabularies in ways that never would have happened if she hadn't created Harry Potter. She's also responsible for reviving the study of Latin in middle schools. Dr. Robert Atkins transformed our approach to diet and health. Steve Jobs was the force behind the first mass-market personal computer, the revival of animated feature films, and a transformation in the recorded music industry. In three different worlds, Jobs demolished the myth that only huge organizations can transform the way we live. Each of these people became fabulously wealthy from their work, but that was the least of their accomplishments.

Bono. Oprah Winfrey. Bill Gates. Warren Buffet. Dolly Parton. George Lucas. Rudy Giuliani. Martha Stewart. These are people who have exerted a immensely positive influence on different aspects of our lives. They are people who prove a key principle of the New Normal: in a technology-driven global economy, individuals can often cut through the clutter better than corporations.

What does this have to do with you? You may not be in a position to replicate the impact on the world of a J. K. Rowling, but you are definitely in a position to have an impact on your own world. One of the paradoxes of the New Normal is that as companies shed employees, individuals become more valuable. They are more valuable in large companies because there are fewer people to do the work, more valuable outside large companies because small companies will pick up the slack. The era of the individual offers great opportunity for each of us.

I was lucky enough to begin my career during the early years of the era of the individual. Nothing was more inspiring for me than to watch a succession of smart, motivated people develop a vision and a goal and forge ahead in uncharted territory. During my days at T. Rowe Price, I watched Warren Buffett, Peter Lynch, and others revolutionize the investment industry. I never would have started Integral Capital without the trail blazed by the likes of venture capitalists John Doerr and Ben Rosen—individuals who embody the spirit of the New Normal. John began as a role model, became a friend, and ultimately my business partner. The Flying Other Brothers would not be around today without the influence of rock musicians who were curious about the convergence of technology and music. Bob Weir, Mickey Hart, G. E. Smith, Jorma Kaukonen, and Jack Casady gave us not only inspiration but also guidance as we refined our sound.

WHEN BIG WAS BEAUTIFUL

For forty or fifty years, everything that mattered happened on a monster scale, with some big institution behind it. From 1940 until the mid-1970s, *big* ruled everything from business to government to religion. People derived their identity and financial well-being from association with large institutions. Everyone knew IBM, General Motors, and GE. Few people could name the people who ran those companies. Big business in that era operated under the command-and-control model that had served the U.S. military so well during World War II. It was a model that favored predictability over efficiency. Layers of management made it possible to control huge enterprises on a global scale at a time when technology was exceptionally primitive by today's standards. American corporations delivered predictable results, but they were inefficient bureaucracies. The model worked because the competition—such as it was—consisted of other inefficient bureaucratic American companies.

While it's hard to pinpoint the exact inflection point when all that changed, the most likely candidate is the winter of 1973 to 1974. That was when the OPEC oil embargo transformed the global economy. Fuel shortages and huge jumps in energy prices undermined the business models of giant American companies, to the benefit of competitors in other countries—especially Japan. In industries ranging from automobiles to technology, Japanese companies stepped to the fore. For the ensuing decade, the American economy struggled to adapt. While the U.S. auto industry has never regained its former position of global leadership, American companies in technology and other sectors recovered well. In many cases, though, the mantle of leadership fell to a new generation of companies. Politics, social change, and new technology all played a major role, empowering small entities to challenge the established powerhouses.

In the end, the bureaucracies of *big* simply stopped being competitive. The world economy had entered a new phase, unleashing both new global competitors and new business models. The inability of many big companies of the day to adapt paved the way for a transformation of the U.S. economy and a spectacular revival of entrepreneurship. Although we didn't see it coming at the time, the phenomenon also cleared a path for one of the key trends in the New Normal: the emergence of the individual.

REINVENTING THE ECONOMY

Looking back, the transformation of the U.S. economy was nothing short of miraculous. Somehow, the world's largest economy went from fat and slow to sleek and fast—forcing millions to change careers in the process—with hardly a misstep and with no social unrest. As a country, we reinvented ourselves on the fly. In the late 1970s a new investment model emerged—leveraged buyouts (LBOs)—to exploit the situation. LBO funds went after dozens of incredibly corpulent companies and removed the layers of fat. CEOs throughout the economy got the message: shape up on your own or an LBO firm will do it for you. Across America, corporate midsections were gutted. The companies that emerged were slimmer and more focused.

Their employees also changed. Technology enabled individuals to become more vertically integrated and allowed companies to shrink. You take an executive, hand him a PC, and before long he's doing the job of both an executive and a secretary. He's also running his own ad hoc what-if analyses with spreadsheets. Thanks in part to the slimming down of corporate America, the economy began a long expansion in the early 1980s that climaxed with the Internet mania of the late 1990s. The economy grew steadily as it transformed and gave new opportunities to wave upon wave of people forced out of Old Economy jobs. Most people never looked back.

The transformation of the U.S. economy took roughly twenty-five years, during which the economy had only two brief recessions. From 1982 to 1999, the economy expanded dramatically, finishing with the spectacular period now known as Internet mania. As the new millennium began, the U.S. economy dominated the world as never before.

Then it all came crashing down. It happened to many of my friends. And just about every person in the economy faced a day of reckoning. The employees who kept their jobs had to pick up the slack. That meant working even harder. Those who got laid off had to find work in an environment in which their past experience might have had only a vague relationship to their future opportunities. The inflated titles of the mania were gone. For many former CEOs and vice presidents, those titles are gone for good.

INDIVIDUALS WIELD MORE POWER

The New Normal has forced each person—employed or not—to rethink his or her role, priorities, and future. Employees who survived the layoffs have discovered they are incrementally more valuable to employers. With each round of layoffs, they've had to assume *more* responsibilities. They have never had so much influence before, but they are stretched to the limit. Every day is like a never-ending exam in which you don't have nearly enough time to answer all the questions but you have to find a way to score high anyway.

If you lost your job, the options have been few, and often disappointing. I have heard this from friends at every level. Even CEOs from failed dot-coms have struggled to find new jobs in the New

Normal. Frustration levels are high. But the worst is over. The economy has begun a new era, one in which individuals are becoming more powerful—and valuable—than ever before. We're now in the era of the individual.

The era of the individual is new, but it will reward many traditional business values. Positive thinking is as important as ever. Regardless of the setting, individuals can make a difference. And most of the things we do have consequences. If the adrenaline rush of the mania caused many of us to forget these time-honored concepts, the New Normal gives us an incentive to remember them.

Back in the first chapter, I told you to write down things that are important to you, specifically things about family, career, and personal finance. Now we're going to put that list to work in the first of our Investor Alerts.

INVESTOR ALERT

The first step in successful investing is to know yourself. Start by determining your investment objectives, time horizon, and risk tolerance. I'll talk more about these things—and how to determine them—in the chapter on investing, but for now the important thing to understand is that investment success is about knowing yourself. Start with your current financial needs and opportunities, and then think about how those needs are likely to evolve over the next ten years. What is likely to happen in your career? What are your family priorities? The next step is to find a strategy that helps you get from here to there. Great investors find a strategy that works for them . . . and they stick with it. They don't change strategies when someone gives them a hot tip. They don't change because of an advertisement on cable television. Neither should you.

Investor Alerts in the chapters to come will help you apply the lessons of the New Normal to your personal portfolio. These alerts are just a tool, not a genie in a lantern. To get the most from them, ask yourself how each one applies in the context of the important things in your life.

When big institutions started losing their power, it was small institutions that gained influence. Suddenly, MCI began playing in AT&T's league. Microsoft and Apple Computer challenged IBM. Federal Express muscled its way into the domain of the United States Postal Service. Nasdaq started to gain ground on the New York Stock Exchange. Southwest Airlines began soaring, while decades-old name-brand carriers dropped like flies. And the entrepreneurs behind each of these upstarts—the Fred Smiths and Bill Gateses and Herb Kellehers and Steve Jobses and Bill McGowans of the world—became cultural heroes. Individuals changed the world, creating a new age of tycoons. They got fabulously rich doing it. Not all of the new tycoons changed the world for the better—Enron's Kenneth Lay and WorldCom's Bernard Ebbers did just the opposite. And on the world stage, after forty of years of fearing the Soviet Union, our country now must deal with enemies such as Osama bin Laden. For good or ill, and in all spheres, individuals have more power than ever.

Recently the era of the individual moved beyond the new tycoons. In the New Normal, the individual is a fundamental building block in our economy. Influence for individuals is the inevitable end result of decades of decentralization. It is also the result of technology. In many ways, the era of the individual owes its existence to the personal computer.

The PC has equipped individuals to perform more and increasingly complex tasks. It gives individuals huge leverage. It provides the power they need to be productive and successful, whether working independently or in the context of small or large enterprises. In the largest enterprises, technology gives individuals the ability to have a greater impact than ever before.

Think about the power of technology. It provides individuals with the same capabilities historically enjoyed by large businesses. It gives individuals access to the same information. And the same tools. It also empowers individuals to project an image previously available only to much larger institutions. Meanwhile, adaptability has replaced scale as the most desirable characteristic a business can have. What's more adaptable than an individual? In the New Normal, the advantage goes to those who are willing to adapt.

THE IMPACT OF A SINGLE INDIVIDUAL

While much of the technology innovation of the past twenty years was targeted at enterprises, the value often came from enabling individuals to do the work previously performed by groups or entire bureaucracies. When PCs first emerged, the core applications—spreadsheets and word processing—provided huge leaps in personal productivity. The leap from spreadsheets to electronic mail and the Internet was every bit as profound. Where the corporations of the 1950s, 1960s, and 1970s required layers of middle management to communicate strategy and maintain control, the corporations of the 1990s could use e-mail and the Internet to accomplish better results with far fewer management layers. With each new wave of technology, the economic opportunity for individuals has grown dramatically.

Adding to the woes of large companies has been a shortage of leadership. While it may not be related, the era of the individual has seen the emergence of executives who are long on charisma and short on basic leadership skills. What passes for leadership today is often little more than a telegenic smile and good public relations. No matter how big a company is today, it will only succeed if its leaders can actually lead. In this age of productivity—where every company is making do with fewer employees—leadership is more important than ever. It all comes down to motivating individuals to do their best, helping them adapt to a rapidly changing business environment.

Large companies have long recognized the impact that a single individual can have at the management level. In the New Normal, enterprises will increasingly recognize the value of individuals at all levels of the organization. The right person in the right job is a powerful lever, no matter the level and no matter how large the enterprise. If you don't believe me, consider the damage that can be done by the wrong person in any job.

This comes at a time when companies want to operate with as few people as possible. Throughout the coming decade, companies will keep headcounts as low as they can—even as the economy improves. As a result, those who are employed today have found their roles becoming even more demanding and more valuable, as each individual is required to create substantially more value. You can look at this one of two ways. You can gripe that they're asking you to do a lot more work and not paying you for it (at least not right away). Or, you might realize that they're giving you more responsibility, which gives you the chance to broaden your skill set and show what you can do. If you believe in yourself, this situation is good news.

Impossible as it might seem, you should view the fact that you're stretched to the maximum as a positive. Over the medium and long term, more responsibility means more opportunities. It will give you more options. Instead of being hyperspecialized, you will gain a broader range of skills. You will have more opportunities to demonstrate your competence. The fact is, when business picks up, companies will reward those who have proved themselves capable of handling increasing levels of responsibility. When I talk to friends who have been successful in business, almost everyone has tales of taking on roles that initially appeared to be uncomfortably large. For most, that situation proved to be a career turning point.

A CHANCE TO PLAY OFFENSE

You can also start looking elsewhere. Having survived the downturn, you're soon going to get your first window to think of the future in the context of the New Normal. And survivors will be the most highly prized candidates. Right now you may be hanging on. But over the next two or three years you are going to get the chance to play offense rather than defense. If you're in a job that's not a good fit, you'll get your first opportunities to make a change. The more successful you are in your current position, the more options you will have with respect to the next one.

It may be hard to believe, but the uneven distribution of power between employers and employees will eventually shift back into balance. Employers have held the upper hand since 2000—it seems like forever—but that won't last forever. A return to equilibrium will create big opportunities. But as more power swings back to employees, it makes sense to be realistic about those opportunities. The key thing to remember: the late 1990s aren't coming back. This won't be a time to take a job with an inflated title in an industry you don't like with people you can't stand doing things you despise in the hopes of getting rich. Last time around you could be forgiven for not appreciating that the safety nets are gone. When you threw it all away to take that job in Silicon Valley the first time, you could be forgiven for getting wrapped up in the fury. Whatever you do now, don't make that mistake again. You're now in "fool-me-twice" territory.

This time, be exceedingly thoughtful about the opportunities that become available to you—and more conscious of risk and return. Again, resist the urge to take a job with an important title at a firm with a questionable future. In fact, don't take any job unless you can imagine sticking with the company over the long haul. While positions will definitely be opening up in the New Normal, we won't be seeing anything like the frenzy of "opportunities" we saw in the gold rush. That's a good thing. You'll have fewer options, but they're likely to be based in reality and therefore more likely to lead to success.

THE VALUE IN SELF-AWARENESS

Self-awareness will be incredibly important in the New Normal. As you consider career options, give consideration to qualitative factors as well as financial ones. Look for a company where there's opportunity to succeed in both the near and long term. Pick a job that suits your skill sets and you'll be more likely to do well. Go to work with people you like. With the slower pace of advancement comes the increased probability that you'll have to stick around in your job for more than a week or so. If you *are* successful, you are going to become indispensable virtually overnight.

If you are unemployed now and cannot find a job doing whatever it was you did before, it's time to rethink your strategy. The New Normal doesn't look like the old one, and you may be one of the people whose only option is to change direction. This is not an economy that's going to support inflexible people. So the trick is to make sure you're flexible.

Despite the trends, there are still holes in the support infrastructure for individual contractors. Health insurance is a prime example. Health insurance for individual contractors is still expensive and hard to obtain. Fortunately that represents a major opportunity. As a group, individual contractors aren't any more of an insurance risk than employees. Some forward-thinking insurance provider will figure out how to pool the risk . . . and build a very successful business from doing so. The opportunity is too big to ignore.

ACCIDENTAL ENTREPRENEURS

In the New Normal, the distinctions between corporate employment and self-employment are diminishing rapidly. The survivors have been forced to be more strategic about their time, more thoughtful about their decisions, and even more committed to work. They've learned to survive in a risky environment. In a nutshell, those are the characteristics of entrepreneurs. And they have been exposed to a lot more aspects of business.

In a way, the New Normal is training us all to be entrepreneurs. Whether you work for a big company or for yourself, the success formula is pretty much the same. The big question is whether or not you are willing to be your own boss, deal with your own benefits, and find your own business opportunities. It's a practical reality that hundreds of thousands of people need to find employment, and for many of them, independent contracting is an economically viable option. But it's not always the right thing for them emotionally. Just because you have the skills to be an entrepreneur doesn't mean you should be one. Being good at organization, strategy, and time management is essential, but it's not enough. You have to want to build your own business. And you have to be willing to live with the uncertainty. Some people live for the thrill of entrepreneurship. I do, but lots of great people don't.

Some people will be forced into contractor roles because it is the only way to get a job. If your options are limited—and the employer's are not—contractor status is likely to be the equivalent of a pay cut. Hot companies such as Google have used contractor status as a way to "test-drive" employees before giving them traditional full-time employment. As the economy returns to normal and demand for labor comes back into balance, one of two things will happen: companies will offer regular jobs to their best contractors or the contractors will be able to raise their price.

Already, self-employed individuals have more opportunity—and leverage—than ever before. Thanks to the Internet, software packages targeted at entrepreneurs, and new wireless technologies, there are few limits on the commercial dreams of individuals. But there are major hurdles. Some are emotional. A fundamental question: Are you well suited to entrepreneurship? If you're considering becoming an entrepreneur and starting your own business, you might ask yourself why you haven't done so already. If the thought of starting over does not appeal to you, you're not likely to succeed as an independent contractor. And some of the hurdles to self-employment are strategic. In the chapter on small businesses, I cover the basics of strategy and business plans.

MASTERING TECHNOLOGY

No matter where you work—alone or within a corporation—technology matters. At the margin, individuals who have the best understanding of the technology available to them will have a huge competitive advantage. In this productivity-crazed environment, you have to learn to be smarter about how you allocate time. Technology can help. But you have to master it if you have any hope of becoming more productive. If you don't take control it actually *wastes* more of your time. That becomes critical as the workday extends into the night and weekend.

For example, just because you've got wireless e-mail and a cell phone doesn't mean you should surrender your life to them. I turn the notifications off on three of my four wireless devices—everything but my cell phone—and I only give my mobile number out to a handful of people. As a result, I check my wireless e-mail only when it's convenient to me.

Self-employed or not, you want to get ahead of the curve in technology. People are impressed by otherwise normal individuals who understand technology. I don't know how long that will be the case, but it's certainly the case now. Being an early adopter makes you more indispensable than the guy next to you—again, this is true even if you're an independent contractor.

Embracing technology doesn't mean you should go out and waste money on it. But pay attention to what's going on. Spend fifteen minutes each day learning about new technology or mastering a technology product. Take an IT person to lunch. Read online articles. Skim through a book. There's literally no excuse for not knowing about technology today. It's not that hard. Unlimited information is accessible. The people who are clever about managing technology to their advantage are going to win.

When your bosses talk about bringing some new technology into your line of work, don't be resistant to it. Be the one who volunteers to help them evaluate or implement it. If you understand the technology, you are almost certain to have a competitive advantage over some meaningful percentage of the people around you. And if you help *them* understand it, you will be far more valuable to everybody.

Being more valuable *as an individual* is what the New Normal is all about. You want to increase your value—and there's no better time to start. You've got the tools at your fingertips. The world is shifting in your favor. And if we've learned anything from recent history, it's this: nobody's going to take care of you other than yourself.

.10.

IT'S A GLOBAL ECONOMY—PERIOD

Before September 11, 2001, Kevin Hickey was lucky if he sold a flag or two each day from United States Flag Store, the online retail business he operated out of his Pittsburgh basement. Within hours of the terrorist attacks, he was deluged with orders—thousands of them each day. Meeting the surge in demand was difficult enough. Then it became impossible: the source of flags dried up when Hickey's supplier opted to sell exclusively to Wal-Mart, which was also benefiting from the resurgence of patriotism.

He found his answer in China. A Chinese flag manufacturer e-mailed Hickey offering to supply him with flags. The manufacturer's products were less expensive than the original supplier and comparable in quality. Now Hickey purchases hundreds of thousands of dollars in flags each year from the Chinese supplier, whom he has neither met nor even communicated with over the phone.

And the supplier offers a broader range of products than his predecessor, a bonus that has enabled United States Flag Store to significantly expand its offerings. Combined with a few other online niche stores he operates, Hickey expects annual revenues to approach $20 million in 2005. That's more than twenty times the business he was conducting in 2002.

I stumbled upon Hickey's story by accident, when I went online to track down an Alaska state flag to give to my wife last Christmas. (Why would a couple born on the East Coast, living in California, want an Alaskan flag? Because it's a really cool flag: the Big Dipper on a blue background.) Hickey's experience illustrates a key characteristic of the New Normal: scratch a flourishing business—any flourishing business—and you'll find a global connection. It doesn't matter what industry. It doesn't matter what size. It can have global suppliers or customers—or both.

If you were to believe newspapers, politicians, and some economists, globalization is a topic for public debate. To me, there's nothing to debate. Globalization is the environment in which we live. We've got one world. Get used to it. Make the most of it. Debating globalization? It's like asking fish to debate the merits of living in the sea.

The reason for the debate is that globalization has been painful in some parts of the U.S. economy. Some communities have been badly shaken by the reorganization of the U.S. economy and outsourcing of jobs to lower-cost geographies. As natural as it is to want to eliminate the pain, we should be careful about trying to stand in the way of the globalization tidal wave. The United States may be the most powerful country in the world, but we can't even control the value of our currency, much less the ebb and flow of world trade. And the truth is, the pain of globalization has been relatively small in comparison to the benefits.

If you live in the United States, globalization has mostly been a good thing. It has been the single most important contributor to low inflation over the past decade. Your dollars go a lot farther than they might have, thanks to low-cost manufacturing in Asia, Mexico, and elsewhere.

Globalization also has increased the choices in consumer goods and services. Where do you think grapes come from in the middle of January? (Answer: Chile.) At the same time, globalization has opened up new markets for American goods and services. Quick. What's the most popular restaurant chain in China? (Answer: KFC.) And lastly, globalization has contributed to rising standards of living in many former members of the third world. Rising standards of living promote order and security. It wasn't so long ago that China was considered a source of instability in the world. No longer.

All of this is due to globalization.

INVESTOR ALERT

The explosive growth in China, India, and other emerging countries has produced big returns for some investors. Are you tempted? The opportunities in emerging markets are huge, but the risks can be very big also. Before you take the plunge, consider that emerging markets are relatively inefficient—both in terms of information and trading activity—and that there may be a home-field advantage for local investors. You may be able to reduce some of those risks by thorough research or by investing through a mutual fund.

Just remember: if the opportunities in China and India are as good as the bulls claim, they will last for a decade or more. A modest investment over a long period of time is likely to be more profitable than a series of short-term trades.

NOT ANOTHER MANIA!

The trouble with globalization is that most people see the phenomenon as either the most positive force in the history of humanity or the most vile. The answer is that it is neither. Globalization is neither the end of the world nor the end of the rainbow. It's one more thing out there, a New Normal phenomenon offering opportunities, risks, and choices that have to be made.

Many people I meet haven't quite detoxed from Internet mania. They're craving another wealth-generating high. For some of them, globalization has become that new intoxicant. It's as if they've discovered a rebound gold rush in Chinese Internet stocks. But just as it's unwise to fear globalization as an economic threat, it's also dangerous to consider it an economic silver bullet. Technology has opened up the planet as a source of labor and products and as a market for goods and services. But that doesn't mean globalization is the ready answer for everyone's sourcing and market needs. There are still businesses that are inherently local. For example, most newspapers are community based. Heavy building materials—cement would be an example—are too expensive to ship very far.

When considering how globalization might affect your business, there are a lot of things to keep in mind. Transportation time and costs matter for most physical goods. (There is an entire economic theory that states that the more advanced the economy, the lighter the goods it produces!) Cultural values are also a factor. Despite the increasing homogeneity of culture around the world, the distinctions still matter, and they create business opportunities for those who understand them. (They also create costly and embarrassing mistakes for those who don't.) You may have noticed that in some corners of the planet they don't play by the same rules we do.

For example, it's hard to buy a legitimate CD in Thailand, Paraguay, or Russia, parts of the world that are notorious for not respecting intellectual property. Or look at credit card fraud. It's rampant in Romania, Indonesia, Macedonia, Belarus, and many other places.

Fear of fraud is what kept the online retailer eHobbies from going global—until now. Seth Greenberg and Ken Kikkawa revived this dot-com casualty, which once maintained a 175-employee workforce and burned through $30 million in venture capital. After the bust, the partners—both former employees—purchased the intellectual property and inventory, working hard to leverage eHobbies' brand to rebuild the business. Today, eHobbies sells 30 percent more hobby equipment than it did at its Internet mania peak, and with only twenty employees. But even as they grew their business, the new owners limited their market to the United States, Canada, and the United Kingdom. "We didn't want to do business in countries where we couldn't get an AVS match," says Greenberg, referring to the address verification system that helps retailers confirm a credit card holder's address. "Until recently, we didn't feel comfortable taking that risk." The owners initially focused on the markets they understood best. That cautious approach served eHobbies well as it sought to create a stable basis of business from which to expand.

When they felt the time was right, Greenberg and Kikkawa took a systematic approach to expanding their market globally. After surveying the possibilities, in spring 2004 they enlisted the services of Comerxia.com, a technology, marketing, and logistics company that helps retailers like Brooks Brothers, Wolf Camera, Amazon.com, and Wal-mart.com link with worldwide shoppers. For a relatively small percentage of the retail price of each product, Comerxia takes the risk out of selling merchandise to customers in unfamiliar territories.

Comerxia does more than help retailers. It also saves customers shipping costs by consolidating products from multiple retail clients into a single package. When someone in Italy orders a model train set from eHobbies, a question appears on his or her screen. (Example: Did you know you can get drugstore.com products shipped in the same box?) After combining products earmarked for a single destination, Comerxia ships the package to a Mail Boxes Etc. or other delivery location convenient to the customer in Italy. The customer takes possession of the package after showing ID and the credit card used to make the purchase. The transaction clears at that point, not at the moment the customer made the online purchase. For Greenberg, the arrangement is a no-brainer. eHobbies can vastly expand its sales territory with no risk of fraudulent credit card orders.

Thanks to companies such as Comerxia, the market has solved a thorny globalization problem: helping retailers overcome their fears of fraud in order to take advantage of a distinctly New Normal phenomenon, the emergence of worldwide demand for just about any niche product you can imagine.

TARGETING JAPANESE CONNOISSEURS

Opportunities exist, but they need to be approached thoughtfully. Adrian Lurssen, a native of South Africa, worked in Yahoo!'s editing department when he struck upon the idea to become an online purveyor of tea in mid-1999. As so often happens with great ideas, he stumbled upon it. His brother-in-law had stopped in at Lurssen's home in Mill Valley, California, to discuss his prospects of finding work. They were sipping tea while they talked. Lurssen, who spent his days toiling in one of the hottest of dot-com enterprises in the world, found himself saying, "Don't get a job, create a job." The next thing he said: "This is great tea. I need to find some more of it."

Their future was under their noses. Americans have a distinct approach to buying tea, he reasoned. There's loyalty to a particular brand, as opposed to a particular type or quality of tea. "We made the assumption that there's no place online to get multiple brands, so we structured an online catalogue," he said. Lurssen and his partner formed allteas.com and signed up for a link on Yahoo!'s shopping site. In the first years, they concentrated on selling existing brands of tea, doubling their sales every year. By 2003 they decided to boost their margins by launching their own line of teas.

Lurssen noticed a trend. Customers in Japan were ordering rooibos (pronounced *roy-boss*) tea, a South African infusion that is popular for its healing benefits. Allteas zeroed in on the market, claiming the territory and creating customer loyalty before the competition could see it coming. "More and more Japanese are buying rooibos, and they're buying it from us," said Lurssen.

Scratch a flourishing business and you'll find a global connection. When he cofounded Aerial Media Services, Inc., in San Francisco in 2001, Max Lodish decided to take a professional approach to an advertising medium traditionally run by small-time entrepreneurs who knew little about the world of advertising agencies. The first thing they did was put up a Web site aimed at media buyers interested in learning about blimps, hot air balloons, inflatables, and other flying media. In its infancy, the start-up's entire marketing budget of three dollars a day was invested in key-word-search advertising. It worked—in an unexpected way. One of the people who found Aerial Media's Web site was an Australian who had invented a means of deploying helicopters to pull advertising banners. He was eager to expand into the U.S. market. Aerial Media wanted another flying medium. It was a match made by the Internet. The two companies have been working together ever since.

My friend Chris Shaw is the artist who creates awesome posters for the Flying Other Brothers and lots of other rock 'n' roll bands.

He works out of his studio in Oakland, California, but you can find his posters in music clubs and homes throughout the world. His venture into the global marketplace owes its success to his Web site, e-mail, and online auctions over eBay. "Before eBay, I was forced to sell posters for whatever the small local market was willing to pay. And I felt ripped off on more than one occasion," he explained.

So from one side of the San Francisco Bay, Adrian Lurssen is selling tea to Japan. From the other side, Chris Shaw is peddling rock posters to aficionados of high-end rock 'n' roll art. "There's a small market of Japanese buyers that specifically collect this type of thing," he said. They buy gift baskets for the parents of newborns, too. Lynne Bingham, owner of The Stork Delivers, has found her baby gifts and accessories are particularly popular among Japanese consumers who order them for shipment to relatives in the United States.

GLOBAL CONSUMPTION BOOM

Procter & Gamble is selling a lot more Tide detergent in Mexico City than ever before. More Pampers, Crest toothpaste, Herbal Essence shampoo, and Bounty paper towels, too. In fact, so much that America's leading producer of consumer goods is in the process of building a massive manufacturing campus in Mexico City that is an unfathomable one million square feet in size—ten times the square footage of the one it replaced and approximately 50 percent larger than Estadio Azteca, Mexico City's 110,000-seat soccer stadium. And the campus's entire production will be consumed locally. That's how much standards of living have risen in Mexico over the past decade.

Contract electronics manufacturer Flextronics has seen a rise in the Mexican consumption of Xboxes and other products it makes in Guadalajara, Mexico. Today, 20 percent of the production stays in Mexico, versus zero in 1996. Output from the company's plant in China's Guangdong province is being snapped up by Chinese consumers faster than last year. Now, 13 percent of the production stays in Asia—up from zero five years ago. Car ownership in China has risen by nearly 37 percent over the past three years.

Lost in the debate over globalization is a key windfall for all nations that choose to participate in the global economy: there's a demand side that is sprouting beneath our feet. Not among Japanese consumers of tea and artwork, but among consumers in places that never have been considered thriving markets for American goods and services. Only a decade ago, China, India, Mexico, and Eastern Europe were barely measurable as markets for consumer products. Today, each is thriving, and each has become an important market for American goods and services.

For so long we've been focused on the supply-side of globalization—the global tilt toward low-cost centers of labor for producing the world's goods—that the whole issue of demand in those economies has felt like a footnote, as if the demand would materialize sometime in the distant future. The general sense was that U.S. companies were saving production costs by manufacturing overseas, redeploying domestic labor to higher-value jobs, and selling some components and equipment to those manufacturing centers. These sales are not trivial, and they are growing rapidly. Keep in mind that every computer sold to India has an Intel microprocessor, a hard drive most likely made by an American company, and software from Microsoft and others. In 2003, India imported $4.9 billion worth of equipment from the United States, up from less than $2.5 billion in 1990. This is not a huge number, but it's not insignificant. And it understates the impact of U.S. technology. While few, if any, of the PCs acquired in India come from the United States, many of the high-value components do.

Well, the demand side has materialized, and it brings with it exciting prospects for improving the global standard of living. In the plus-sum game that is globalization, growth in per-capita income in developing nations creates demand for products. That includes demand for local products as well as the unique output of other economies—for example, the movies that Hollywood pumps out so much better than anyone else. In the New Normal, companies are succeeding with products and services you never thought you'd be able to sell in places like China. One example is life insurance, a booming market, pioneered by Aetna in 1997, that shows no signs of ebbing. Another is KFC, which I mentioned earlier. KFC now has more than nine hundred restaurants in China and opens a new outlet every other day. In the trade, KFC is "aspirational" dining. Why? Chicken has been an expensive delicacy in China. By providing great-tasting chicken at affordable prices, KFC tapped into a deeply rooted cultural vein. Besides, it's "finger-lickin' good."

Demand among Chinese consumers for KFC, life insurance, automobiles, and everything else creates more jobs, but it also shifts the center of gravity of the Chinese economy. Increasingly, production in China is being diverted to satisfy local demand. That means that less of China's output will be exported, suggesting that the worst of the Chinese outsourcing threat may be over for American industry. Rising local demand in a vibrant global economy creates a virtuous cycle that improves incomes and lives around the world. Globalization is like a stepladder.

TEMPORARY DISRUPTIONS

The challenge of globalization is to bring new countries into the fold, first as a source of supply, then as a source of demand. The essence of that is education. Why is India booming? The key to India is that you have a humongous population of exceedingly well-educated people. China, Mexico, Brazil, and other nations are working to imitate India's success. There's no question the world is better off having these nations as productive members of the global economy. If we want to improve our competitiveness, we, too, should follow India's example. There is certainly ample room to improve education in the United States, particularly in primary and secondary schools.

This transition from closed-loop national economies to an open-loop global economy is an extremely positive shift. Developed countries can do well by helping emerging countries do well. As with change of any sort, there are disruptions. We're not going to get this right on the first pass. But we eventually will.

Globalization makes the world one huge market. While this means that economic activities ultimately will be more evenly dispersed around the world, it also causes disruptions. Thanks to globalization and technology, governments that once were accustomed to calling the shots are finding it increasingly difficult to influence their populations. Influencing economic policy at home or abroad is even harder.

It has been politically attractive for some to dwell on the temporary disruptions of globalization. Americans have been losing jobs to foreign manufacturers the way they had lost them to machines or competing regions in previous generations. There's an irony in the billboards along South Carolina highways that read: "Lost your job to free trade or offshoring yet?" A generation ago, South Carolina was gaining jobs at the expense of states in the northeast. We've lost jobs to globalization the same way we lose jobs to technology, business restructuring, public policy, and changes in consumer tastes.

I'm very sensitive to these concerns. But I'm also aware of the limits of public policy in a global economy. Economies don't stand still. They evolve continuously. Global economies do so in ways that no government can control. Ironically, that situation is actually very good for us, as the United States has been the biggest beneficiary of globalization among the established world powers.

The political problem with globalization is that the benefits are spread across the entire population, while the pain is concentrated in a handful of communities. A small number of people are bearing the burden so that everyone else gets the benefits. This doesn't seem fair. But the right answer is not to restrict trade or try to protect jobs. Protecting industries is a shortsighted approach. All that does is spread the pain.

When we protect an industry from competition, we are imposing a cost on everybody else to protect a small number of people. It's a lesson the Bush administration learned when it used tariffs to try to protect jobs in the U.S. steel industry. Ultimately, we lost more jobs among customers of the steel industry than we saved in the steel industry.

So when a business becomes uncompetitive, we have two choices. We can either penalize the whole population to benefit a small number of people, or we can help that small number of people do something to help not only themselves but also everybody else. The big opportunity in the New Normal is to help those who lose their jobs. Support retraining. That is a lot better for the economy and a lot cheaper than protecting their old jobs.

DEBATING THE INEVITABLE

Opponents argue that globalization is a bad thing. Among the criticisms: it exploits cheap labor in developing countries. As much as I would like to solve all of the world's problems in half a generation, I don't think that is realistic. Per-capita incomes and standards of living are rising throughout the developing world, and I have a hard time believing that working people in those countries would be better off if their income and standard of living were not rising. It is certainly true that income is not evenly distributed in emerging countries, but the same is true in this country. Education is one of the secrets to better income distribution.

In nations like Mexico, India, and China—which have been supplying labor—standards of living have risen very rapidly, but from a low level. Both countries still have large numbers of people living in poverty, but far fewer than a decade ago. Based on current trends, the ratio of "haves" to "have-nots" will improve significantly in the years ahead.

Another major criticism of globalization: it hurts the environment while taking advantage of working people in less-developed nations. It's true that less-developed nations are generally more focused on improving their standard of living than they are on preserving the environment. But that tack doesn't last very long. As standards of living rise, so does concern for the environment. And the environment, it turns out, is very resilient. Just think about the water quality improvements to the Hudson River over the past generation, or the air quality in formerly smog-choked cities like London or Pittsburgh or Los Angeles. Besides, it hardly seems fair for us to suggest that emerging countries not work to increase their standard of living. We had our turn. Now it's theirs. In this country, and in every other country, once the standard of living hit a certain level, people started to care for the environment. When they did, recovery followed.

Meanwhile, I disagree with the notion that the United States is even in a position to decide whether or not globalization continues. If that was ever true—and I suspect it never was—it's not true now. In the global economy, countries can do what they want. Look at Indonesia, which, for the most part, has chosen not to participate.

And I'm not suggesting that the entire planet needs to import American culture. I'm suggesting that the New Normal frees local economies from the paternalistic, protective infrastructure that severely limited choice—not to mention, opportunity. Once communism evaporated, globalization was the best case. The alternative was to have huge parts of the world be depressed and threatening the economic and political security of the rest of the world.

Whatever the flaws are in globalization, it has some enormous benefits beyond economics. Just consider the World Health Organization's unbelievably effective response to SARS. It's a great example of globalization rippling into the governmental sphere.

MANAGEMENT FACTS OF LIFE

What does this mean for managers? The issues for managers are really simple. Think of it as an equation: management equals execution, where execution is a function of technology plus globalization. Technology and globalization are facts of life for business, and the idea that one could be a good manager and not be conversant in technology and globalization strikes me as ridiculous. Those are the new languages of management.

In the same way that you evaluate technology, you have to evaluate global markets as sources of supply and demand. From the supply side, that means expanding your view of the world: learn how to create pools of trained labor to accomplish certain tasks in appropriate geographies. Learn about the markets of talent. Learn about what can and cannot be relocated. Assume nothing, test everything.

The reality is that it is easiest to move commoditized activities associated with business processes that aren't going to change much. When you take an operation that is a commodity in California and move it to India, you reap multiple benefits. It's not just that the labor costs are lower, but the occupancy costs are less and the health insurance is less. You have a markedly lower cost structure. This has been true for nearly a decade. I know this because we invested in our first company that conducted software development in India in 1996.

However, whenever you shift work overseas, the communications costs are infinitely higher and management becomes exponentially more complex. To that end, there is huge risk in shifting high-value activities that are sensitive to communications. Wars have been started based on a misplaced comma in a telegram. Managing across time zones and language barriers is difficult—at least one party to every conversation between India and the United States has to be awake in the middle of the night. That gets old very fast. And then there's the risk that the politics or economics change radically in the country with which you're doing business.

Meanwhile, as I indicated, the opportunities on globalization's demand side are staggering. Recent success in globalization was primarily about lowering manufacturing costs. The next ten years will be about increasing sales and profits in an environment where the tide is gently rising. Those profits might be lurking in an unexpected corner of the globe.

It's important to keep in mind that not everything is going to export uniformly. You have to experiment, and you want to experiment when it costs relatively little to do so. You have to be smart about it. You have to be sensible about how you test. Yum Brands did all that in China. They experimented with KFC, Taco Bell, and Pizza Hut. KFC worked best. They found local people and trained them well. Then they invested heavily. Success!

And remember: it's not a land rush. The New Normal is about being sensible, taking appropriate risk, and having appropriate time horizons. But you can start today.

I have this recurring vision of a consumer in India or China or Mexico searching frantically for a copy of *Finding Nemo* and not being able to track one down. The world market is swelling with promising new sources of demand. And somebody will have to satisfy it.

That might as well be you.

.11.

INNOVATION—AND EVERYTHING ELSE—MOVES TO THE EDGES

The New Normal is about the ultimate in decentralization. I call it innovation at the edges.

Information technology's first wave took place in air-conditioned rooms where IT professionals—and only IT professionals—labored over applications that helped organizations manage their information. The second wave pushed computers out of the air-conditioned rooms and onto the desks of company employees, where PCs linked in networks deployed client-server applications. Suddenly nontechnical employees were moving the data and crunching the numbers.

The third wave of information technology is about the edges, where technology touches the real world. The architecture is called Web services, and it enables companies to collaborate with their customers and suppliers. Web services first appeared just before the new millennium and triggered a tsunami of press at the time. The press was overblown and grossly premature. But over the next twenty years, Web-services-based innovation at the edges will transform business and our lives as dramatically as the mainframe and PC waves . . . and quite possibly more so.

INVESTOR ALERT

One of the challenges of technology investing is the press coverage of innovation. The press loves new technologies, and tends to describe each one as the greatest thing since sliced bread. The early promoters of innovation collaborate in this hype because it eases the challenge of raising capital to fund their work. The problem is that only a handful of the heavily hyped innovations fulfill their promise. This is bad news for investors.

If you want to avoid getting bagged by promoters, focus on *products,* not concepts. If there are products, there must be a business model. If there are products and a business model, investors can judge the attractiveness of the business. The early promotion of Web services focused on applications called "B2B," which means "business-to-business." The idea of collaborative applications was brilliant. The problem was that there were significant holes in the underlying technology that made it more or less impossible for B2B collaboration to work at that time. As a result, the much-promised benefits of B2B required a miracle to occur. It didn't. What made the situation particularly challenging for investors was the willingness of enterprise customers to pay up for promises. When the products didn't work, the backlash was huge. Billions in market value disappeared, and some B2B vendors went out of business.

Five year later, the press has forgotten about Web services. It's old news. But for investors, Web services is only just beginning. Some of the biggest holes in Internet technology have been filled. Over the next five years, most of the rest should be addressed. This is the time for investors to be learning about Web services. The investment opportunities today are relatively few, but they will grow in number and attractiveness as we move forward from here.

Obviously, there still are a lot of mainframes and servers in air-conditioned rooms and PCs on enterprise desktops. And that technology still has an important role to play. But it has stopped changing the business world. The next wave of technology extends beyond enterprise firewalls. It extends out into real life. That's where the people are. That's where the dollars are. It's where the future lies.

What do I mean by real life? Real life takes place in homes, in stores, and everywhere that people meet. Technology is transforming real life. Airport check-in kiosks have eliminated one of the many lines associated with air travel. And that's just the tip of the iceberg. As it evolves, Web services will become a platform for connecting existing enterprise technology to the real world, reducing inventories, improving forecasts, and saving time and operating costs. In combination with peripheral devices such as Radio Frequency Identification (RFID) tags, Web services increasingly will help retailers and their suppliers put exactly the right product in the right place at the right time to make a sale. Biometric, tokenless payments will speed the checkout process and release a flood of information linked to the fingerprint of a human thumb.

Significant gains in productivity and lower costs are just the beginning. Businesses will be able to know more about their customers and their own operations than ever before. Thus businesses will be vastly more flexible. And they will be able to offer new levels of convenience to customers.

For consumers, the innovations will make life easier and better. For managers and business owners, the new technology creates thrilling opportunities for experimentation. For investors, it opens up vast new territories: companies that sell the new technology and companies that improve their operations by deploying it wisely.

It also stands to trigger an avalanche of privacy concerns.

As you put more technology out at the edges of the network, a nagging question hangs in the air: what happens to all the data? We're approaching a world in which it's cheap enough to compile a storehouse of data involving your every transaction and your every movement. A big database of everything you do might be immediately accessible to virtually anyone. What happens then? Each of us is entitled to our own trade-off between convenience and privacy. What is industry's responsibility with respect to privacy? The answer will be hotly contested in the years ahead. Again, the First Amendment right to free speech will clash with the Fourth Amendment right to privacy. We'll also face mounting security concerns.

EVERYBODY'S A GEEK

The Web services architecture depends on the Internet for its foundation, and it represents the next level beyond e-mail and Web sites. One of the key building blocks is the Extensible Mark-up Language (XML), which enables applications at the edge to communicate with each other, as well as with the legacy computer applications on which most companies run their business. One of XML's key attributes is flexibility. Where earlier generations of technology tended to produce applications that did not allow for change, XML assumes the need for adaptation. This is a very big deal.

As the Web services architecture matures, applications will enable collaboration among business partners. Imagine the automation of enterprise-to-enterprise business processes, with no human intervention. An example? Inventory replenishment. When the Web services architecture is mature, a retailer will be able to deploy a system that will monitor inventory and automatically send merchandise orders to suppliers at the appropriate time, while the system at the supplier's end automatically triggers the corresponding shipment. Armed with this technology, retailers would run out of merchandise far less often than they do today . . . and more customers would find what they want to buy. (It's worth noting that in 27 percent of out-of-stock situations, the merchant actually has the merchandise in the store but just can't find it. Technology can help.)

Today, processes such as inventory replenishment require lots of people and time—with corresponding costs and operational inefficiency. Because the infrastructure for two-way collaboration is still pretty primitive, the applications being deployed are generally automated on only one side (either vendor or customer, but not both). Your bank can automate bill payment on their side, but you still have to input the amounts and approve the transactions.

The innovation-at-the edges trend will encompass a range of technology advances—everything from RFID tags to biometrics to mobile videophones. Such devices will translate the real world into streams of digital bits, but they are only a piece of the Web services story. Think of them as input devices akin to a keyboard, a mouse, or a point-of-sale terminal. At the edges you need lots of input devices. The real challenge is to support them with software that makes the applications compelling. It's the glue that allows collaboration to happen. Capturing real-world data is important, but the true value is in what you do with the data. That's why software is the area I find most fascinating, and most promising for long-term benefits.

INVESTOR ALERT

Every time a new architecture comes along, its proponents forecast a revolution, promising to replace legacy systems. Sometimes that happens, but more often new technology gets applied to business processes that had not previously been automated. When PCs and workstations came along, they didn't replace mainframes. When the Web services architecture is ready for prime time, it won't replace PCs and workstations. Nor will it replace client-server applications. SAP and PeopleSoft will have to find new avenues for growth, but there is almost no chance that customers will rip them out in favor of Web services. Once installed, enterprise applications typically last until it becomes economically unfeasible to maintain them. Thanks to Y2K and other initiatives, the cost of maintaining client-server applications is modest compared to that of replacing them. If Web services is going to be as big a deal as I expect, it will be the result of new categories of applications—and collaboration will be a feature of those applications.

Why do you need a new architecture to enable collaboration? There are two reasons. One is that the old architectures—mainframe and client-server—weren't designed for collaboration among enterprises. They were designed in the days when most companies were vertically integrated, when the requirement was to manage internal business processes. The cost of implementing Web services applications with client-server technology is not generally practical. If you are willing to spend a fortune—as Wal-Mart has—you can get amazing collaborative functionality out of mainframe and client-server technology. But that's not how the masses will do it.

The second reason is that corporate priorities have changed dramatically since the early days of client-server. Flexibility is what enterprises want today. They want to do business with fewer employees. They want to outsource everything they can. Companies believe that if they can automate collaboration with business partners—without adding people to their payroll—they'll walk away with the pot of gold at the end of the rainbow. Client-server does not deliver flexibility. Web services will.

For this to work, though, Web services has to enable ad hoc secure collaboration. The goal is to provide transaction capability that has the convenience of Amazon.com's OneClick ordering system, which enables registered customers to buy products with a single mouse click. Ad hoc functionality is essential because companies need to have the flexibility to change their supply chains and distribution channels as often as necessary. A supplier on one project may be a competitor on the next one. Companies can't let their business partners—even the ones they trust—wander through their most important data files. That's where security comes in. The architecture of mainframes and client-server depends on firewalls to maintain security of corporate data. And firewalls are to collaboration with business partners what chastity belts are to sex.

TEN YEARS OF INNOVATION

Like the mainframe and client-server waves before it, Web services will continue to evolve during its first decade, stabilize, and then begin a long period of tremendous growth. We are only four years into this timeline, so we can expect incredible innovation through at least 2010.

At some point over the next five or six years, Wall Street will probably fall for another mania, this time about Web services. Investors want to believe in a Next Big Thing, and one can sense that they are ready to hyperventilate about RFID. The reality is that the next five or six years will still be part of the development stage of the enterprise Web services business. It will be a period of experimentation. A few systems will work. Many others will fall short. And the big money won't be made until standards are set and best practices have been developed. Once that happens, everybody—vendors, customers, and investors—will prosper.

Here's how it will happen. The focus today is on creating tool kits. The tool kits will enable enterprises—and contract software developers who work with them—to craft applications to automate specific business processes. Many of these applications will not work effectively, either because the customer does not really understand its business processes well enough to automate them or because of limitations in the underlying technology.

But some applications will work, and the vendors that craft them will gain business advantage. Others will take notice and adopt a similar approach. For some the approach will work, but the rest will continue to experiment. This cycle probably will last four or five years, at the end of which we'll see the first packaged applications software based on the best practices that emerge from the cycle of experimentation.

The early adopters of that packaged software will have problems with it. As with the tool-kit-based custom applications, the early packages will have bugs and limitations. But within a few years, both vendors and customers will have worked through the kinks. At that point, the market will move from early adopters—enterprises for whom the desire for competitive advantage outweighs the costs and challenges—to the early majority. This is when everyone—including investors—gets really rich.

INVESTOR ALERT

Major new technology industries typically develop in three distinct phases. The first phase is infrastructure, which is typically a physical layer of hardware. In the PC industry, motherboards, semiconductors, and disk drives are examples of infrastructure. The second phase is enabling technology, which typically consists of software or protocols. In PCs, the best example is the operating system. In combination, the infrastructure and enabling technology form a platform. This platform supports the third phase, which consists of applications, content, and services.

There are two profoundly important aspects of the three-phase model. First, the phases happen sequentially. It is not unusual for infrastructure to be around for years—even decades—before the key enabling technology comes along. Only after the enabling technology is reasonably stable is the platform suitable for applications, content, and services. When new markets emerge, investors often try to jump the gun by investing in phase-three businesses before the platform is stable. This strategy generally ends in disappointment. The key insight is that investors should focus on stage-appropriate investments. In the early days of an industry, infrastructure is where the opportunities are. Later on, enabling technology is where the action is. Only when the platform is mature is it possible to make money in applications, content, and services.

The second important aspect of the model is that the value of winners in each phase is very different. Infrastructure businesses tend to be relatively more capital-intensive than businesses in the other phases. Competition can also be pretty fierce. Enabling technology, by contrast, is a natural monopoly. Customers insist on standards, which means one winner per category. In PCs, Microsoft was the big winner, but not the only one. Intel's x86 microcode, Adobe's PostScript, and Apple's Macintosh operating system are successful enabling technologies on the PC platform. Profit margins for enabling technology tend to be very high, so once an industry gets big, the players tend to be very highly valued. Phase-three businesses tend to be more competitive—and less profitable—than enabling technologies, but the revenue levels can be huge. As a result, the biggest winners in phase three can make you lots of money, but only when an industry is well established. The big winner in PC applications was also Microsoft, and the numbers didn't get big until the mid-1990s. At that point, Microsoft had been selling software on PCs for fifteen years.

Keep in mind, though, different enterprises—and vendors—will be ready for Web services at different times. You'll hear lots of hype. Don't fall for it. Whether you're a potential customer for the software or a potential investor in the vendor, be wary. Look beneath the surface to make sure that what you are looking at is real. And really valuable.

CONSUMERS GET THERE FIRST

The best examples of Web services today target consumers. eBay is probably the best known of these, thanks to the millions of participants in its marketplace. eBay has technology for automatic bids and overbid alerts, which are simple examples of Web services at work. As an eBay customer, you set bidding guidelines that the system will manage for you automatically. It's a one-way form of automation because it requires you to check your e-mail to be certain that the bidding is still inside your range.

The first two-way consumer Web service that I became aware of is TiVo's digital video recorder. I'm a big fan of Cary Grant and Katharine Hepburn, and I can program TiVo to record every TV program that includes them. After that, I don't need to do a thing. My TiVo communicates with the central server automatically and will then fill its hard drive with movies featuring Cary Grant and/or Katharine Hepburn. I can watch the movies whenever I like. The same concept has been implemented by Netflix for its DVD-by-mail service. Customers give Netflix a long list of movies they want to watch. Netflix sends out a new movie from the list each time the customer sends back one he or she previously ordered.

There are many reasons why Web services showed up in the consumer arena first, but the most important one is that it was relatively easier to deliver good value. When enterprises make purchases, different people—generally different organizations within the enterprise—are responsible for specifying the product, making the buy, deploying the product, and using it. Enterprises need to have rules and procedures to make sure that capital is invested wisely and that new capital investments provide an appropriate return. This requires people, procedures, business processes . . . and complexity. Making consumers happy is so much easier.

Meanwhile, one of the lessons learned from the first two waves of information technology is that industry standards are essential to the success of any new architecture. Standards lower the cost of technology, both at initial purchase and in long-term support and maintenance. The Internet has an excellent selection of tools and protocols—you may be aware of http, XML, and the like—but they were designed for the current environment of Web sites and consumer transactions. More work needs to be done to enable automated collaboration between enterprises.

There are numerous projects under way to adapt XML to the requirements of collaborative applications, but that work will take more time. Until the new communication standards have been completed, it will be both costly and time consuming for companies to deploy Web services to collaborate with suppliers and customers. Just as important, the business processes related to this collaboration differ from company to company. No two companies manage their supply chains the same way. As a result, I expect the pace of new applications deployment to be slow for at least the next few years. That said, I expect lots of experimentation.

A REASON TO EXPERIMENT

Companies have a huge incentive to experiment. Why? Because it's not enough to deploy just any technology in your business. As I noted earlier, older technologies such as mainframe and client-server can help improve your cost structure, but that's it. If you want competitive advantage, you have to deploy the latest technology, and today that means Web services. Being an early adopter of technology is hard work—and sometimes painful—but that is how the most successful companies stay ahead. Early adopters generally experiment on a small scale. They like to see that a technology works before they make big investments.

Web services will certainly help companies get the best price when they buy and sell, but they will also provide a foundation for better business processes. For example, Web services may enable companies to rethink their supply chains and their distribution channels. This will take time, and it may be five to ten years before enterprises capture the true benefits. Again, you should expect that different companies will realize benefits at different times.

INVESTOR ALERT

Selling new kinds of software requires vision, which is always much neater and clearer than reality. Vendors will tout their solutions and the returns on investment that come with them. In a market with several players—all with a compelling vision—it's often hard to tell which company is likely to win. At the very beginning of a major wave, it's generally possible to invest in multiple players in the same segment, simply because it will take a few years before they actually compete head-to-head. In most software categories, at least one company has a technically elegant solution, whereas at least one other vendor has a "quick and dirty" solution. Once head-to-head competition begins, I almost always bet on the quick and dirty solution. The reason is that the real world is not technically elegant, and quick and dirty vendors are generally more willing to do what customers need. When Apple introduced the Macintosh in 1984, it had a technically elegant solution in comparison to Microsoft's DOS. But Apple resisted market input, thereby giving Microsoft a chance to catch up . . . and then grow to its current level of market dominance. In databases, Relational Technology and Sybase had elegant products, but Oracle used a quick and dirty approach to win out over them both. This happens in every new industry.

Web services will create endless opportunities for companies to work together with customers and suppliers, but success will require new approaches. For one thing, operating executives will need to be much more closely involved in the purchase and deployment of Web services than they were in the mainframe and client-server waves. Information technology professionals may understand the technical side of Web services, but it is the operating people who understand the business processes to be automated. If companies want those processes to be implemented in a way that is flexible, operating people are going to have to partner with IT people as never before.

The operating people who touch customers and suppliers are not accustomed to having technology available to automate their processes, and they are going to have to step up to the challenge. Experimentation is essential. This means that no one should accept a software vendor's promises at face value. Silver bullet solutions are few and far between. In the real world, software—especially new software—is quite limited in what it can do.

There's very little standardization from company to company of the business processes for handling purchase orders, requests for proposal, and the like. Without standard processes, there can be no standard applications to enable automation. Without standard applications, there won't be big winners on the vendor side, at least not at first. Why? Think about it. Every purchasing officer probably thinks his or her company gains competitive advantage from its unique purchasing processes. They will hesitate to jettison their winning business process to match a vendor's software.

Only through the development of standard solutions—applications—at cost-effective price points will there be an incentive to abandon unique approaches. The move to standard software is always painful—as SAP's customers learned in the 1990s—so it generally takes years to gain the confidence of customers. It worked for SAP and its customers. It will work in Web services. But in Web services, it won't happen any time soon.

What needs to happen first is that the industry develop a broader suite of standard protocols for collaborative commerce. Then vendors need to develop or adapt tool kits to support the development of custom solutions based on those protocols. There has been a great deal of effort expended in both areas, but it only scratches the surface.

It's hard to make money in protocols. Almost by definition, protocols must be in the public domain so that no one can control them. (A few vendors—Microsoft and IBM are examples—have been able to maintain proprietary protocols, but that is the exception.) So the big near-term opportunity on the vendor side revolves around tool kits. Three companies are particularly well positioned today: BEA Systems, IBM, and Microsoft. Each got its start by selling a product known as an applications server, which is basically a tool kit for creating applications on the Web. Each of these vendors has built a big customer base, and each has a vision for the future. Applications servers are a good starting point for the Web services wave, but today's products are far more primitive than what I envision for the long term.

On the customer side of the equation, the availability of tool kits will support experimentation. Given the very early state of the industry, I don't expect any two companies to experiment in the same way. However, I expect everyone to benefit from the experimentation of others. Each time an experiment works, it will give competitive advantage. Because the advantage will come in business processes that touch customers or suppliers, it will be obvious to all and will invite imitation.

Imitation will ultimately lead to standardization of business processes, which in turn will enable standard applications software. The pioneers will have some setbacks, but the competitive advantage they gain from their early successes is likely to be very large. As others imitate, these companies will move on to the next area of automation, extending their advantage. A well-managed company that presses its advantage will be able to sustain it for years.

NEW OPERATING SYSTEMS

When I use the term *operating system,* the image that probably leaps to mind for you is Windows or Macintosh Operating System X. These operating systems are based on a file system. The file cabinet metaphor works very well for a world dominated by spreadsheets, presentations, and word-processing documents. For a Web-dominated world, however, file systems fall short. In a sea of content, search is a better metaphor than hierarchical file structures. When you look at the new services on the Internet, many of them are based on search. Friendster and LinkedIn are examples. Now think about the situation in your own home. Does your PC hard drive have photos on it? Recorded music? Video? The file system on today's PCs does a pretty horrible job of helping you find what you need in content files . . . even the ones on your own PC.

As the Web services wave crests, I anticipate big changes in the operating system environment. Windows and Macintosh OS X will not go away, but they have to evolve into managers of digital data. They have to incorporate search. Apple does this in partnership with Google. Microsoft will do it in competition with Google. Either way, customers are better off.

One of the really interesting questions is how search will evolve in the world of Web services. The value of search is not so much in the indexing of content, but in the presentation of search results. Tightly matching results to the customer's query is essential. Doing so in a way that is easy to use is compelling. The next step will be to create applications that leverage the search model. The opportunity is huge.

EARLY ADOPTERS WIN

Web services won't be the only area of corporate information technology to expand in the New Normal, but it will be the most ubiquitous. For the near term, the revenues will be dominated by early adopters.

Microsoft never could have launched its XBox on retail shelves in time for the 2001 holiday season without the ability to collaborate on complex design and manufacturing processes over the Internet. By relying on Agile Software's Product Collaboration suite of software, Microsoft could concurrently engineer the XBox with Flextronics, the contract manufacturer that was responsible for manufacturing the video game hardware and getting the box into stores in a tight time frame.

Microsoft also collaborated over the Internet with two hundred other vendors engaged in the design process. Flextronics' and Microsoft's supply-chain partners were able to review XBox design changes and swap real-time design information in a Web-based workspace. It won't be long before that technology appears primitive, but at the time it was very innovative . . . and it made a huge difference to the success of the XBox.

Agile's software is an early example of the potential of Web services, but its capabilities focus on engineering change orders, just one of dozens of business processes within supply-chain management. There are unique aspects to the management of engineering change orders that contributed to Agile's success. So far, no equivalent solutions exist in any other segment of the supply chain today. Eventually there will be.

Ace hardware, a $2.9 billion cooperative with over fifty-one hundred independent retail members, uses Web Services to collaborate with twenty-two suppliers on planning, forecasting, and replenishment. Among the suppliers is Manco Inc., the manufacturer of duct tape and other adhesives. By using software developed by JDA Software Group, Ace and Manco share a real-time view of sales by product and store, as well as a joint sales forecast.

In that way, both companies can reduce inventory at the same time they ensure there's the right amount of duct tape on the shelves. In its first year of operation, the collaborative effort has lowered distribution costs by 28 percent, reduced freight costs by 18 percent, increased annual sales by 9 percent in a flat category, improved forecast accuracy by 10 percent, and increased human productivity by more than 20 percent.

As you read about companies deploying Web services to streamline supply chains and shave operating costs, you undoubtedly are eyeing them as companies potentially worthy of your investment. Keep in mind that the move to Web services isn't likely to make the difference for a company that is poorly positioned or poorly managed. The technology alone isn't enough to make the company a good investment. The Web services architecture is no more a silver bullet than the mainframe or client-server architectures were.

.12.

TIME IS A SECRET WEAPON

This image says it all. It's 2001 and you're coasting down the freeway behind a tow truck that's repossessing a late-model Porsche, bearing a bumper-sticker that reads, "Stop for Lunch and You *Are* Lunch." Remember Internet Time? The New Economy was taking over everything and the business world as we knew it—the Old Economy—was toast. Pets.com would blow away Petsmart. Webvan would blow away Safeway. Everything would be different, and all that mattered in the new economy was that you had to be there first. It was akin to the conceit of *Field of Dreams.* If you could create a brand, customers would materialize. You could get from zero to insanely huge in no time flat. That's when people worked virtually around the clock in the hopes of getting rich quick. Except for Mark Cuban and a handful of others, most people wound up with little to show for their investment in time other than pink slips, faded prospectuses, and T-shirts from failed dot-coms.

They also were left with something distressing: a seriously warped view of time.

The sprint that was Internet mania is over, although some survivors I meet still operate as if it's more important to be first (at anything) than to be right. And they can't seem to focus beyond the next eighteen months . . . or eighteen minutes. That is not a good way to plan or manage your career.

For about a three-year period, everybody raced against the clock and expected things to happen quickly. And things did happen quickly: companies made their entrance and exit in a hallucinogenic blur. The perception was that you had to move quickly because that's what winners did. It certainly is true that Netscape, Amazon.com, Yahoo!, and eBay had all moved fast. And their founders were all phenomenally rich. The message was: a gold rush has begun! With an entire economy to reinvent, the opportunities were unlimited, but time wasn't. The big bucks would go to those who got there quickly.

Reality turned out differently. Being early mattered. But moving fast hurt more people than it helped. In retrospect, it's clear that most of the people and businesses that succeeded during the Internet mania were those that took the time to make the right planning decisions.

It turns out that neither companies nor individuals had to move at lightning speed. The concept of Internet time was a misreading of the factors driving the success of early leaders such as Netscape and Amazon. The idea gained credence when entrepreneurs, venture capitalists, and investment bankers saw the quick returns possible with Internet Time. Almost overnight, it provided an excuse to cut corners. It was easier to act without much planning. For a while, it was more fun, too.

But take a look at the companies born in that era that are actually still around—and flourishing. They mastered their business. They stayed focused. They got enough capital at the right time. It's ironic, but the companies that emerged successfully from the Internet mania operated in pretty traditional ways. The same is true for successful people.

Yes, despite all the hype, the old rules were still in force. Cash flow and profitability mattered in a major way. Not during the mania, of course. But when the mania ended, it didn't take long for the cream to rise to the top.

Sure, those who are successful always move faster than their competitors. They have better internal processes. They make *good* decisions faster than their competitors. The essence of success in the business world is not to move *absolutely* fast. It's to move *relatively* fast. Remember the joke about the two guys in the woods when the bear shows up? As one guy starts running, he asks the other why he's taking the time to put on sneakers. The fellow replies: "I don't have to outrun the bear, I only have to outrun *you*." In the real world, you don't have to set a record; you only have to outrun your competitors. Making a decision today is helpful only if you make the correct decision.

One of the Internet pioneers—Netscape—prided itself on its ability to move at Internet speed. Netscape was spectacularly innovative, and at one time it was the hottest company in Silicon Valley. Thanks to its groundbreaking browser software, Netscape had the first Internet portal. For a while, Netscape also controlled Internet search and even had the leading applications-server software. Recognizing that Microsoft would be a serious competitor, the executives at Netscape knew they needed to build a defensible position. The result was that the company decided to focus its energy on the market for corporate e-mail. The problem with this decision is that Microsoft was the market leader in e-mail, and they basically pounded Netscape into the ground.

Netscape might have fared better had it concentrated on segments where it was strong and Microsoft was weak, namely in the Internet portal business, Internet search, or applications servers. Unfortunately, Netscape did not see the potential in those markets. As an early proponent of Internet Time, Netscape made decisions quickly. Would taking more time have led to better decisions? It's hard to know. With the benefit of hindsight, however, we can see that the markets abandoned by the now-defunct Netscape produced huge success stories such as Yahoo!, Google, and BEA Systems.

For all the rushing around during the Internet mania, it's worth noting that being late was not the barrier to success that most people thought. Late arrivals at the Internet party—including Blue Nile in jewelry, and Google and Overture in search—were among the biggest winners. Their success can be attributed to thoughtful analysis and exploitation of a market opportunity that was being missed by others. Google and Overture realized that search was second only to e-mail in the ranking of Internet applications. It offered a unique opportunity to provide pay-for-performance advertising, which Overture innovated and Google exploited. So while the perception was that available time had shrunk, it really hadn't—at least not with regard to the opportunities that mattered most.

To be clear, it is better to be early than late. But it is always more important to be right than to be early.

INVESTOR ALERT

On Wall Street, they say "Timing is everything" and they're right. Timing is critical to investment success. Everyone knows that being too late is bad for your investment results, but did you know that being too early is, too? As my partner

Jim Davidson likes to say, "Being too early is the same as being wrong."

Any time you hear something exciting about a stock, ask yourself at what point in the news flow you are hearing it. If, for example, you read a story in the *Wall Street Journal* or heard it on CNBC, you have to assume that lots of people are hearing the same thing you are. At that point, the opportunity depends on having an insight not readily available to others. For instance, consider the news that Intel has decided to change its strategy in 64-bit microprocessors. The news stories make it clear that Intel has been forced to act by a combination of its own product problems and competitive alternatives from Advanced Micro Devices. Intel's stock immediately goes down a little, while AMD's goes up a little. While the news sounds big, it isn't, as the issues with Intel's 64-bit chips have existed for a couple of years, and investors have just been waiting for Intel to admit them. It's already too late to make money on the news itself. To make money on the stocks after the news comes out, you would need to have an insight about AMD's ability to take advantage of Intel's problems, or about Intel's ability to recover from them. This same model applies to any investment situation. The next time somebody offers you a tip on a hot new technology concept, ask yourself what has to happen for the concept to generate a billion dollars in revenues. The hot concept these days is nanotechnology. It sounds great, and perhaps it will be a huge market one day. But that day is years—and possibly decades—away. This is not to say that you cannot profit from trading swings, but only that your timing must be very precise, and the risk of losing money is very high.

DESTINATION VS. JOURNEY

During the Internet mania, time was like a beam of light with a single focus: *Can I get rich in one or two quarters?* In the mania environment of the late 1990s, it seemed as if everybody was focused on reaching the destination—wealth—as quickly as possible. Management teams and venture capitalists began to focus on building market capitalization rather than on building companies. The focus on wealth became a cultural norm to the point where stocks and stock options became standard topics of conversation at cocktail parties. It's not that the journey didn't matter but rather that everyone thought it would be a short one. And there was tremendous excitement in being part of an economic revolution.

People put their nonwork lives on hold—and in extreme cases uprooted their lives—to be part of it. Few people reached their intended destination, and far too many found themselves out of work or in situations with limited long-term prospects. Not only did those people not achieve their goals, they didn't enjoy the journey. At least not the last part of it. Don't make that mistake now. In the New Normal, the happiest people will be those who optimize their lives across multiple dimensions. They will find a sustainable balance among job, career, family, and personal interests. Remember that life is about what happens along the way. The journey matters.

If getting rich is a priority for you, that's great, but be realistic about the time frame.

One of the problems with the goal of getting rich is that it often requires a single-minded focus. Single-mindedness gets old pretty fast. It's hard to enjoy the world around you. It may even be difficult to appreciate the fruits of your actions. And you may not be the most interesting person to be around. If you've weighed the consequences, and riches are still what you want, go for it. But remember that a full bank account without a full life isn't much of a life at all.

INVESTOR ALERT

The end of the Internet mania provided investors with costly lessons about speculation and risk, but the market recovery that began in late 2002 triggered a bit of amnesia. Momentum investing and speculation have returned, at least temporarily. I love bull markets, but I do not welcome this development. I would hate to see a repeat of late 1990s investor psychology. One of my favorite sayings is, "Always make new mistakes." This is a variant on the aphorism "Fool me once, shame on you; fool me twice, shame on me." If you want to be a successful investor, it's absolutely essential that you keep score on everything you do. Successful investors recognize patterns in data and news, and this appears to give them the ability to see over the horizon. What's really happening is that they analyze not just the data and news but their own reaction to it. In this way, they minimize the emotional component of decision making. They learn from their mistakes and do not repeat them. They make only new mistakes.

If the Internet mania was about getting rich overnight, the New Normal is about living well for the rest of your life.

Where the Internet mania was a sprint, the New Normal is a marathon. Time horizons should be longer, affording the opportunity for deliberate decision-making, due diligence, and planning for life beyond the next couple of quarters. This is great news because one of my tenets has always been "The guy with the longest time horizon wins." Most people optimize around their own short-term self-interest. This can work well, but it's not the only option. It turns out that a longer time horizon allows you to see opportunities—and to make choices—that can lead to very favorable outcomes down the road. Think of a longer time horizon as an investment in yourself.

TIME AND SPENDING MONEY

The environment of the New Normal provides incentives to be strategic about your life and to balance short and long-term considerations all the time. You need to consider the trade-off between what makes you happy or successful this afternoon, versus where you'd like to be in the future. When setting your priorities, remember that this afternoon is brief. The future lasts for years.

This has always been true, by the way. There's nothing new about suggesting that investors think in terms of the long haul—and devote time each week to working toward goals you hope to achieve next year, in five years, in twenty years. But the pace of change over the past five years has left too many people with the impression that planning is futile. Not true. Plans and priorities are the best way I know to relieve stress.

Consider the example of a new car purchase. As fun as it would be to upgrade your car today, ask yourself what would happen if you invested the money instead. How would your life change? Can you imagine things you might value more in five years than a new car next month? I have consciously made this trade-off hundreds of times over the past twenty years. And only once did the new car win. That was back in 1992, shortly after I moved to California. I bought a new Toyota Camry, which I still drive today. I'm not a car guy, so my trade-off may not apply to you.

Some people find it uncomfortable to defer consumption. It's hard to be a saver when the people around you are spending. The American dream of home ownership—and a house full of *stuff*—is very tempting. And it may be the right answer for you. But perhaps not. You won't know if you don't make an explicit analysis. As you do your analysis, don't forget to think about risk and stress. If you borrow a lot of money to prefund your American dream, be prepared for stress later on. It's worth thinking about this before you borrow the money.

I believe the New Normal will reward you for extending your planning horizon. This applies to many elements of your life: your career, your job, your family, where you live, and how you operate your business. The idea is to be specific about your long-term goals and make sure that every major decision you make contributes to them. For example, my wife, Ann, and I always planned in four-year and eight-year increments. Four years was the time between academic sabbaticals, which made it ideal for career planning. One of the central issues in this planning process was our long-distance commute. We committed to it four years at a time. In our world, four years was near term. Eight years was long term.

Pick a time frame that suits you, but I would recommend something greater than three years. You need a longer time for an investment to earn a payoff. When you invest in yourself, don't be tempted to flip your own stock.

The same is true of businesses. Say you do a start-up. If the start-up survives the first five years, you will almost certainly witness the transition of the start-up from nothing to a viable business that has a solid foundation. But for most start-ups, the early years will not make you rich. The second five years are when the business can take advantage of its solid foundation and grow rapidly. During this period, you have a shot at making pretty good money, but even that won't be the big payoff. It is during years ten through fifteen that things get really interesting. If your business is a success, that's when you'll reach significant scale—and make spectacular money. That's how wealth creation works in the real world. Startups are fun. But successful ones take time to work.

TIME AND YOUR CAREER

In the Old Normal, you hunkered down in your foxhole until some paternalistic executive reached down, pulled you up by your lapels, and set you on a path that would convert your job into a career. He plucked you from the ranks and volunteered you to attack the front lines. If you were good at following orders and managed to avoid alienating your colleagues, you flourished. If not, you were stuck. You watched the world pass you by.

Sure, this is a vast oversimplification, but it helps illustrate a key point: In the Old Normal, you didn't have a lot of control over your career. For the most part, other people pulled the strings. You likely had job security, but relatively few real options. Think of the New Normal in terms of Superman's Bizarro World, where everything's in reverse. Now you've got zero job security but countless opportunities. You've got lots of decisions to make. And, again, nobody's going to tell you what to do. Or, just as important, when to do it.

What you have to do is pick your head up and peek outside your foxhole and keep track of the environment around you. Continually expand your skill sets and contacts. You will, in effect, be setting your sails for when the best opportunities start gusting in your direction.

Right now the value of looking up from your foxhole is huge. There are a lot of choices out there and lots of opportunities. But not all good opportunities are obvious. Just as important, the choices don't come at predetermined times. That's why you have to keep looking up. Opportunities never sweep in when it's convenient. In fact, they always seem to arrive at the moment of maximum inconvenience.

The first step in career optimization is self-analysis. Know yourself. This was always necessary, but it's more important in a time like the New Normal, when the plethora of options—and the need to make decisions—creates lots of opportunities for mistakes.

Take yourself out to the beach and ask yourself the following questions:

- What do I like doing? (If you answered "surfing," send me a postcard from your favorite beach.) What do I not like doing?
- What do I do well? What don't I do well?
- Of the things I like doing and do well, what is valued in the economy? Of the things I like doing and do well, what is not valued in the economy?
- What can I do to make myself more valuable? Am I at the best place for me to be doing that? If not, where would the things I do be more valuable?

If the answer to any of these questions is, "I don't know," you aren't looking up enough from your foxhole. Run through this checklist on a regular basis. Do your best to strip the emotion out of it and be analytical.

After you answer these questions, identify portions of the economy that reward your strengths and interests. Learn everything you can about them. Talk about them with people who are already there.

Don't be shy about this last point. If you are truly suited to a particular business, that fact will be obvious to those who are involved in it. Even great businesses need fresh blood.

MANAGING TIME

Many of the people I meet lose track of the distinction between a job and a career. A job is something that pays your bills. A career transcends individual jobs. It is the sum of your professional life. The key is that job and career stop being the same thing after you've been working for about five years. By then your job should have morphed into a career. If not, it's time to stick your head out of the foxhole.

When you start your first job—or any job—your priority must be to focus on what's expected of you and to excel at it. After you develop confidence in what you do, you will have a few cycles of energy left over. You can apply those extra cycles to activities that transcend your job and prepare you for the next phase of your career.

When you begin to feel productivity kicking in, when you get to the point where you don't need to spend every moment of your day just to stay current on your job, when you're starting to feel in control, that's when to begin expanding your horizons. You optimize your career by devoting energy to activities that go beyond the requirements of your job. For example, you might join a professional association or volunteer to work on a company project that does not directly bear on your job. In investment management, it's not uncommon for young professionals to pursue the Chartered Financial Analyst (CFA) certificate. That involves three years' worth of exams, and more hours of study than feels natural, but it makes a difference at the career level. The CFA certification establishes an investment analyst or manager as having a level of professional competence beyond the run of the mill.

When I was at T. Rowe Price Associates, I volunteered for a variety of jobs—recruiting, handling some of the firm's key brokerage relationships, and working on new projects. None of these tasks was related to my day job, and I had to make sure that they didn't detract from my daily performance. But doing them paid huge dividends in my career. In early 1990, I realized that my extracurricular efforts had taught me everything I needed to know to start my own investment business. That wasn't why I did them, but it was a happy consequence. Starting Integral Capital Partners changed the direction and upside of my career.

Also, think about volunteering for activities nobody else wants to do. Why? Just like business school students, most people want to participate in the areas of work where success has recently been achieved. By gravitating to the areas that people shun, you may find yourself amid the future hot areas. You get good exposure and meet people in different contexts. You're actually enriching yourself. If you have an interest in entrepreneurship, it's immeasurably valuable to learn every aspect of your business on somebody else's nickel.

YOUR EARLY WARNING SYSTEM

When you pick your head up out of the foxhole, one of the things you have to do is scout around for relationships of trust with a network of peers and mentors. These are incredibly important. The main reason: there is only so much that you can learn on your own. While you might enjoy learning by trial and error, the reality is that you probably don't have time for that. You learn from experience. Why not leverage the experience of others?

It's an incredibly wise investment of time.

There's no doubt about the value of developing relationships of trust with peers and mentors—it can shorten your path to success, help you refine how you judge people and situations, and provide precious feedback. Relationships of trust can affect both your job and career in profound ways. But they aren't a gimme. The path to developing and maintaining a network of peers and mentors has pitfalls for the unsuspecting. It takes time—trial and error—to learn whom you can and cannot trust. You should never expect people to put your self-interest ahead of theirs. And like all good relationships, business relationships take work. Both sides must perceive benefit in the relationship or it will fade quickly.

The differences between peer relationships and mentoring relationships are smaller than you might think. But you have to have both because they accomplish different things. Peer relationships tend to be most valuable in real-time situations. Because of shared interests, peers are your primary network for keeping track of what's happening now. At a minimum, peers are an early-warning system; they help you deal with the environment you're working in.

Your peers are no fools. You and they may have some common interests, but there may also be some areas in which you compete. To maximize the value of the relationship, there has to be a quid pro quo. You give something to your peer. Your peer gives something to you. It may be a heads up or just a friendly ear when they need somebody to talk to.

When it comes to professional relationships, I always believe in taking the first step. And I don't expect an immediate return. In most cases, I don't expect any return at all. When I take the first step, I know there will be people who take advantage of me. I don't worry about that. I recognize that taking the first step has two huge benefits. It helps to build my network faster because people always want to work with those who are generous with their time and ideas. And some people will return the favor, possibly in ways that are exceptionally valuable to me. With relationships of trust, a return on your investment of time may take awhile, but it will come. The key here is that you cannot make a relationship of trust happen or pay dividends at the moment you need it. You must invest in it ahead of time.

And you have to be realistic about the conflicts that can arise. Depending on your organization, there are some situations in which you can expect peers to be teamlike and other situations where you can't. The culture of your workplace will tell you what your relationship should be to the people around you. It's important to work in a place where your style matches the culture—you don't want to waste months or years trying to adapt to an alien environment.

Even if your culture is intensely competitive, find points of common ground where you can be cooperative with your peers. The goal is to find whatever slivers of commonality exist—and nourish them. People will like you better. In a den of vipers, people will like better the viper who's one percent easier to get along with than everyone else.

It's just as critical that you cultivate relationships with peers outside your organization. They scout the external landscape. And, in combination with your internal peers, they'll ultimately prove to be more valuable than your network of mentors. Mentoring relationships break down when you get to a level at which a mentor's experience is too specific and no longer applies to you. Also, when you become a CEO you may not have a mentor to talk to anymore. In both cases, your network of peers fills the void.

LEARNING FROM OTHERS' MISTAKES

If peer relationships are an early-warning system, mentor relationships are a way to gain the benefits of experience without making lots of mistakes yourself. Mentors can pass along important life and career lessons. If you want to have a relationship with a mentor, you need to be comfortable interacting with a person who is higher than you in the food chain. In some cases, your mentor may be your boss, in which case he or she will have power over you. Either way, it's really important to learn how to have balanced relationships with people who are at a different level than you. My theory on this is simple. Treat everyone well all the time. Whether I'm dealing with a CEO or a secretary, I treat everyone with respect and try to make sure that they get some value from their interaction with me.

Forget the notion of having a single mentor who guides your career. More is better. Having a boss who is willing to mentor you can be a real plus. If another senior person takes an interest in you, that can be valuable in a different way. Why do you need more than one mentor? You don't want to put all your eggs in one basket, especially if that basket is your boss. The more relationships you have, the greater the benefit of their experiences and expertise. But you have to be careful to filter the insights passed on by mentors to make sure they fit your situation. The best way to do this is to develop the relationship over time. Don't be in a rush. And don't be too needy.

Mentoring relationships need to be consistent with your organization's culture, just as is the case with peers. You need to understand whether you're in a firm that by nature is hierarchical—with inflexible chains of command—or one that encourages more of a matrix model, where you can communicate comfortably with multiple people. In the New Normal, the latter is gaining popularity. There's a wide range of cultures in our economy, and hierarchies are not as deeply entrenched as they were in the past. In the Old Normal, things tended to flow down through the organization. Today, there are a lot fewer one-way relationships; everything moves in a mesh. This is a big positive for career-building relationships.

As with peers, there must be a quid pro quo. With mentor-bosses, you work hard to help them succeed in their job. With other mentors, it could be a matter of sharing insights. But in all cases, you provide psychic rewards. Most people like helping others advance. You need to understand what motivates the mentor. With that knowledge, you can ensure that mentors get what they need from a relationship with you.

The most challenging mentoring relationships are those in which you are a direct report to your mentor. If you're a direct report, your mentor controls your upside. Because you're contributing to your mentor's success, he or she might not want you to leave the nest. Not every mentor-boss will step aside to let you move on when you feel the time is right.

I've had a collection of mentors who helped with different aspects of my career. Often, I made the first move by approaching them. But I always had something of value to offer—like a point of view or industry knowledge that could help them. My relationship with the venture capitalist John Doerr at Kleiner Perkins Caufield & Byers began with simple exchanges of insight. I helped John understand the public market for technology stocks. He helped me understand venture capital. Three years later, John backed John Powell and me in the launch of Integral Capital Partners.

INVESTOR ALERT

Where do you get your investment ideas? Mine come in from a variety of sources. Most of the best ideas come from people I know and trust, but some come out of the blue. But I can't remember the last time I made an investment just because some source told me to. I always do my own research. My theory is that I'm the one whose money will be lost if the investment goes bad, so it might as well be my research that causes me to invest.

The starting point for building your personal network is your immediate circle of acquaintances. As attractive as it would be to have the likes of Warren Buffett or the CEO of General Electric as a mentor, people of that status are probably not available to you. No problem. Whether or not you realize it, you are surrounded by people with good ideas and valuable experiences. Your job is to give them a reason to share their ideas and experiences with you. If you bring something to each and every relationship in your professional life, good things will happen.

You need to develop effective professional relationships with all the people who influence your career. You should do the same with people outside your organization whose experience and advice can become beneficial. This will help speed along your career. But always remember: the relationships have to be bilateral.

Another thing to remember: a J-curve runs through the New Normal. That's when you invest more than you reap in the early stages, but in the long run you get paid huge dividends. Because you control how much time and effort you put into the relationship, you can determine how much or little you want to invest. You won't be able to predict *when* a relationship will be valuable to you—or even if it *will* be valuable to you—but if you invest in enough relationships, the payoff will be huge. My best relationships began with no expectations on either side. They just happened. When relationships work, the payoff is in something more precious than money: time. Investing in relationships of trust today takes time, but that time is dwarfed by the time saved and opportunities gained later on.

Just as your mentor might not always have your best interest in mind, the same is true of your employer. When thinking about the trade-offs of job and career, remember that your employer's objectives may be different from yours. Your employer may be happy to see you be the world's expert in a narrow domain—the business equivalent of a character actor who plays the same role in movie after movie—but it's probably not in your interest to be typecast. Do everything in your power to broaden your skill sets. Great employers help their employers do this. Even if your current employer doesn't reward you right away, it will increase your value to future employers.

If you are lucky enough to be in a position where others look to you as a mentor, be generous with your time and experience. In the New Normal, it is hard to predict the sources of great insight. Young people have a perspective that may be very valuable to you.

PLANNING FOR THE LONG HAUL

The important thing about planning is to be realistic about both time and opportunity. Careers develop over fifteen or twenty years. You need a goal and a plan. Your goal and plan may change with time, but they will guide you. When I was beginning my career, I sought out role models. These were people I admired whose careers provided an illustrative roadmap—and a timeline—for me. It's really hard to reverse engineer the career of another person, but it's a straightforward way to gain insight about the strategies and skill sets required for success. Whatever your chosen field, try to identify people whose careers can provide a model for yours. The point is not to match the progression exactly but to have a benchmark against which to compare your progress.

The key is to recognize that every industry has its own rules and culture. In some industries, such as aerospace, companies expect employees to be with them for decades. In others, such as advertising, you have to change agencies to move ahead. Whatever the industry, you have to know the rules and culture before you start. If you want to succeed, you have to fit in first. Success within the system is a prerequisite to doing your own thing. Only when you have proven your abilities will most employers give you the latitude to be different. If being different is your true calling, make sure you pursue a career—and take a job—where being different is valued.

Really good employers understand the importance of developing well-rounded employees. They give their employees opportunities to change jobs internally, in the process gaining experience and perspective. In this era of hyperproductivity, breadth of experience is a huge advantage. It's also more fun.

When I took my first job at T. Rowe Price, I was excited about being an investment analyst. I also knew that the career progression at T. Rowe Price began with research but that the real upside came with promotion to portfolio management. It was a classic "walk before you run" situation. I had been a history major in college and found the notion of being paid to do research very appealing. But research at T. Rowe Price wasn't the same as research in college. For one thing, I had to contend with the stock market. I had done a little investing before and during business school, and I knew I liked the game aspects of investing in stocks. But that was pretty much all I knew when I took my first job. Once I started, I quickly discovered that there are almost as many styles of investing as there are investors.

I spent the next three or four years figuring out what kind of investor I was. I did this by doing my job as an analyst and also by spending every free moment talking to other analysts and investors about the market, their experiences with it, and their views of how to succeed. My first goal was to become a solid analyst. That took me four or five years. Then I had to learn to be a portfolio manager. That took another four. Then I had to learn to be an entrepreneur. That took three or four more years. There were many setbacks along the way—the crash of 1987 and the market collapse in 1990 are prominent examples—but each time I picked myself up and got back on track. By the time the market collapsed in 2000, I had a strong sense it was coming and acted accordingly.

As you consider your situation, be explicit about your own plans and priorities. But also be honest in your self-assessment. The farther along you are in your career, the narrower your set of options. This is not to say that your options are less attractive than they are for a younger person, but only that time has eliminated some choices that you might have had earlier in your career.

FREE AGENCY IN THE NEW NORMAL

So what do you do if your career plan doesn't work out? It's really important to have a contingency plan. In the New Normal, labor relations in the world of business have followed a pattern similar to major league baseball. Prior to the 1970s, baseball players were the property of the team that signed them, which had complete control of the player's career unless they made a trade. Thanks to Curt Flood and others, the balance of power between baseball players and team owners has shifted dramatically, to the point where players have enormous long-term control of their careers.

The business world has started along the same path, as formerly paternalistic employers are becoming increasingly short term in their employment practices. The degree of loyalty from company to employee is much lower now than it was twenty years ago. Today, the balance of power favors employers, but that condition is not permanent. Eventually, the relative power of employees will increase. Unfortunately there is no way to predict when that will happen. The timing may not be soon enough for you. If you find yourself on the wrong end of a disappointing conversation, a contingency plan may be the difference between a soft and hard landing.

In a free-agent economy, employees should take nothing for granted. If your employer demonstrates loyalty, you should respond in kind. If not, you must act to protect your self-interest. I'm always surprised by how many people believe that if they simply hunker down and do their jobs, they're immune from career setbacks.

You need to know what is going on. It will help prevent you from wasting time in a job that lacks upside potential. Even if you have no desire to change jobs, you should understand the broader business issues affecting your company, as well as your part of it. Doing your job well may not be enough to protect you if the business itself has problems. If business or competitiveness deteriorates, your employer's loyalty to you is likely to deteriorate. Perhaps dramatically. It may be in your interest to act preemptively. To do this, you need to be prepared. You need to have a plan—and a backup plan—ready to go. Again, I'm saddened by how many of my friends have learned this lesson the hard way.

The adage that knowledge is power still holds up in the New Normal. Thanks to the Internet, there are more tools than ever for staying in touch with your company's and industry's business. You can use tools such as MyYahoo to automate news gathering on your company and competitors. You can use company Web sites and Monster.com to track hiring in your firm and its competitors. In a mere five minutes a day, you can stay on top of the issues that will foretell any dramatic changes—and give you a head start over people who are not paying attention.

One of the intriguing aspects of time in the New Normal relates to career duration. The baby boom generation and those that follow it will probably work at least five years longer than their parents. The economy is going through a major transformation, the inevitable result of which will be new businesses and new job descriptions. With a little creativity and imagination, you will be able to reinvent yourself from time to time, enriching both your life and your bank account. To do that, though, you have to know what is happening around you.

In a rapidly changing world, some things may happen sooner than you expect. But you should never count on good stuff to happen quickly. It is my experience that everything good takes longer than you would like. You have to allow for that.

The uncertainty of the New Normal has some decidedly positive aspects to it. Maybe in the end it's best to think of life in the New Normal as being a lot like the market for growth stocks. We've traded the security enjoyed by our parents for volatility. Volatility means uncertainty, but it brings with it the potential for a tremendous upside—much greater than was available to our parents.

.13.

WINNERS ARE ALWAYS CONNECTED

The bus carrying my rock 'n' roll band is barreling down Interstate 5 from Seattle to Eugene. The world outside the windows is a blur of soaking greenery. Inside, one band member is watching *Pirates of the Caribbean* on a portable DVD player. Another writes lyrics on a laptop. Still another edits chapters of a book. A fourth talks in hushed tones to his wife on a cell phone. A fifth is downloading digital photos from our performance at the Burning Man festival into a Tablet PC. Other bands in other buses might spend their time partying to loud music. We're not quite of the same demographic. Our priorities are different. When we are not playing music, we are likely to be interacting with screens and communicating digitally. All of us are doing this in real time and all without wires.

I'm the band's leader, and I also try to lead when it comes to technology devices that keep me connected to the universe beyond the Flying Other Brothers. (In reality, technology leadership belongs to Bert Keely, who plays guitar and sings vocals in the band and is also the architect of Microsoft's Tablet PC operating system.) If you could see me now on the bus—or even in my office—you'd notice four wireless gadgets dangling from my belt. In no particular order, they are: Research in Motion's BlackBerry, Danger's Sidekick, Handspring's Treo 600, and a Motorola StarTac phone. I'm test-driving the future—something I do every year or two—to determine which personal technologies work best for me. Coincidentally, I hope to get a sense of whether any of these products is good enough to justify an investment in the shares of the company that makes them.

My little experiment gives me access to virtually anything I need at almost any time. It also gives the important people in my life several options for reaching me. As the bus rambles down the interstate in the steady rain, I'm not missing a beat, businesswise. I'm communicating investment decisions to a colleague, participating in an eBay auction, responding to communication from various investment partners, writing these very words—which I'll submit before we arrive in Eugene.

I never intended to be an early adopter of the permanently connected lifestyle. It happened by accident, but it has served me well. As I mentioned earlier, my wife and I took jobs in two different states, too far apart to commute on a daily basis. On top of that, my work required a heavy travel load. We could only spend weekends together—something we were prepared to do for a time—but we had an unbreakable rule: we would have a meaningful conversation every single day in which we discussed everything important that happened to us during that day. At that time, cell phones didn't exist yet, and my schedule of constant travel typically caused

Ann to have to sit by the phone waiting for my call. It was stressful for both of us. It was also not a life most spouses would choose.

Then Skytel nationwide pagers entered our life. Paging meant freedom. Ann could attend musical performances or faculty functions without fear of missing my call from Dallas or Denver. We were able to page each other to signal our availability. First, with Skytel's numeric version; later, with text.

Still burdened with student loans, we didn't have a lot of extra money to spend on what was, for the mid-1980s, expensive, cutting-edge technology. But we did it. Wireless communications is one of many things I found more valuable than a new car. In some months we were the largest individual users of the Skytel network—not that this distinction earned us any frequent-flier miles. The expense was well worth it. We maintained a wonderful relationship that has flourished for more than two decades without sacrificing our careers.

Here's what else our accidental venture into leading-edge telecommunications delivered. It vastly reduced my level of stress. Knowing that I could contact my wife whenever I needed to, and that she could contact me, I felt more relaxed about my travel. That made me more effective at work. People at work started to link the two—how by stabilizing my communications at home I had become better at my job—and adopted Skytel themselves. Soon, T. Rowe Price moved to Skytel as a standard, which meant they paid the bills.

ON YOUR BODY, ALWAYS CONNECTED

Today, powerful but inexpensive chips, better batteries, and clever use of wireless spectrum mean that wireless e-mail and wireless Internet access are quickly becoming a reality for anyone who wants them. In combination with cell phone advances, these technologies will be absolutely critical to running a business or maintaining strong family ties. They are the tools that can help you get a leg up on one of the pervasive fears of the New Normal: concern about the forced mobility and unpredictable hours required in many jobs.

If you're like most people, you haven't yet seen the wisdom of investing both the money and the time spent learning that are required to become continuously connected. It's up to you, but I think the moment has come to rethink the situation. Be an early adopter of wireless voice or data, and think of your family network as the driver. Get a wireless lifeline that you keep on your person and is always switched on. Eventually, this form of communication will become as commonplace as the landline telephone now is. If you get there before the masses, you will be better off for it.

When we are not in contact with the important people in our lives—family, in particular—stress levels go up. Way up. For everyone. Families that develop a culture of availability all the time are happier than those that do not. Each member of the family is accessible within a few seconds. Stress levels go down. Then, once you've done this at the family level, you will suddenly start to see ways to use it professionally. If the strengthening of family ties and reduction of stress aren't enough to sell you, consider this: by taking the plunge now, you'll gain a competitive edge at work.

The ability to be there when customers, employees, and others need to reach you will be a critical factor for success in the New Normal. By taking advantage of emerging technology, you can make yourself more available than the next guy. As business moves from local to global, from nine-to-five to 24/7, and from batch to real-time, the rewards will go to those who can be reached. Woody Allen said 90 percent of life is just showing up. Let me update him: 90 percent of business success in the New Normal will be just being there when a customer tries to reach you. The same goes for family. You have to be there for them.

Think of it not as a cost in the New Normal but rather as an opportunity.

RAISED EXPECTATIONS

The progression has been at work for years. Until the 1960s, most stores were open from ten in the morning to around five in the afternoon. By the 1980s, when shopping malls had set the standard, lots of stores stayed open until 9:00 p.m. Then, in the late 1990s, people started discovering that they could conduct business whenever they felt like it over the Internet. That raised customers' expectations about business hours. People wanted to be able to order that new CD or check their bank account status when it was convenient for them—be it at 10:00 p.m. or 6:00 a.m. Their expectations were being set by such experiences. And each time they found a service that was more convenient than that of its competitors, they gravitated toward it.

This can work to your advantage. If people feel they can get in touch with you more quickly than the other guy, they're likely to opt to work with you. This is true whether you work in a big company or for yourself. It's true for colleagues and for customers. Often, it's the uncertainty about whether people can reach you that creates tensions in business relationships. Eliminating this uncertainty eliminates tension and sends a strong signal. By allowing yourself to be reachable, you communicate your commitment to colleagues and customers. As a result, others are more likely to trust you.

They don't always need to reach you—just knowing that they can is often enough. And when they do need to reach you, they don't always need a response from you—just the knowledge that you received their message. That alone can ease the concerns that keep people up at night. You've probably been in situations where you needed to get a message to the right person, but didn't necessarily require that person to take any action. ("The meeting schedule has been confirmed by our customer. See you in London on Tuesday.") Because you knew the recipient read the message, you were able to stop worrying about the situation for a few days. Just knowing that you can gain access to someone is enough.

The trick is to become just slightly more accessible than the people you compete with. It will be acknowledged. People will see you as being easier to work with and more committed. They'll want to do business with you.

INVESTOR ALERT

These days, real-time financial market data is so readily available—on the Internet, on television, on wireless devices—that it's easy to get overwhelmed. The key is to recognize that data is useful, but not as useful as information, which is data in context. "One hundred degrees" is data. If the context for the data point is the temperature in Phoenix, that is information. If the data point refers to your body temperature, that, too, is information. What is normal for Phoenix is a fever for you. That is context. Getting appropriate context for investment data is one of the keys to success. Unfortunately, investment context can have many variables. Revenue and earnings growth are not absolutes. You need to know investor expectations to have context. Guidance for the future matters also. In many ways, investing is a game. But the stakes are real money.

SETTING LIMITS

Back when most people had to be in their office to use the computer or answer their telephone, it was highly intrusive to provide such accessibility. Now, with wireless technology, it's possible to be more available without destroying your life in the process. If you're not accustomed to being in touch with anyone you want, anytime you want—and few of us are—you may require a period of adjustment. With some planning on your part, the transition will go smoothly, and you will find yourself on the leading edge at a time when being there is very valuable.

So, if the first step is to invest in wireless technology, the second step is to educate your customers, employees, and colleagues about the best way to communicate with you. For me, it's e-mail. I have major issues with voice mail, starting with the annoying fact that most people leave messages that are far too long. You listen to the person rattling on and on, and then they finally leave their callback number at the end. I call that "receiver-unfriendly" technology. Life's too short.

I literally train people to send me e-mail. I do this by responding quickly to the e-mails they send. They get the message that I'm more reachable this way. They rarely bother with voice mail. And the great thing about having access to e-mail via a wireless device on your body is that whenever you have a free minute you can go through your in-box and check to see if there's anything you need to deal with. You'll know that the thing you need to deal with is there—and you can do it in a minute that would otherwise have been wasted. You respond to the others when you have the time. This point is really important. The secret to making this lifestyle work is control. With wireless technology, you can gain levels of control over your life and career that you never had before. But you need to control how you use it. The payoff is potentially huge.

When you decide to add wireless e-mail and Web access, you gain enormous leverage. Both BlackBerry and Good Technology (the software on Handspring's Treo) integrate with Microsoft Outlook, which means they support the full suite of e-mail, calendar, and contacts from your office. If you're like me, you get so many e-mails at work that notification of each and every one on a wireless device would overwhelm you with beeps and/or vibrations. So I turn off all notifications on my wireless data devices. I check messages only when the time is right for me. This strategy may work for you also.

ADDING HOURS TO YOUR DAY

In an environment where the economy increasingly focuses on individuals, it stands to reason that individuals must have tools that leverage their time. In the military, they call this kind of leverage "force projection." In the New Normal, where we are all pressed for time, force projection is essential. The day isn't getting any longer, and we need eight hours for sleep and a certain number of hours for family and leisure. If we can leverage the hours we devote to work, we will not only be more successful, we will have more time for family and leisure. Technology—wireless technology in particular—is the key to force projection for individuals.

In the economy of the New Normal, competition is very different than in the past. Individuals now play a huge role in the competitive mix. In large companies—where productivity is the mantra—every remaining job is bigger and more important. At the same time, small businesses—including ones with only a single employee—enjoy more opportunities than ever, thanks in large part to the force-projection capabilities of technology. In a world that values flexibility above all else, individuals are the epitome of flexibility, particularly when they are always connected.

You can become more productive. Now you can reach people by phone as you fly from New York to Los Angeles, answer e-mail from the backseat of a taxi. Technology allows you to work a lot smarter than ever before.

Wireless communication has a cost, but it allows you to do more. If you do more, you may be happier, which is good for your family life. You may also be able to earn more, which is handy when the wireless bills come in. The good news is that the cost of wireless devices and services just keeps falling. But the benefits remain as great as ever.

Okay, so we're at exit 195 of Interstate 5, approaching Eugene. It's still raining. This exit has the full menu of life on the road: Denny's, IHOP, KFC, McDonald's, Taco Bell, Taco Time. It's also the exit that will take us to the Best Western, where we'll rest up for tonight's gig. I'm not going to wait until we check in to submit this chapter. I think I'll send it now. . . .

.14.

24/7 IS THE NEW NORMAL

Here's a typical schedule from the peaceful, fairy-tale 1950s:

Midnight to 7:00 a.m.: sleep
9:00 a.m. to 5:00 p.m.: work
6:00 p.m. to midnight: family time

Here's what it looked like in the late 1990s:

8:00 a.m. to 8:00 p.m.: work
8:00 p.m. to 8:00 a.m.: more work

And now it's more like this:

Midnight to 7:00 a.m.: sleep
7:00 a.m. to midnight: work/family time

Technology, the global economy, and the obsession among companies to boost productivity are conspiring to reinvent the clock.

On the surface, the U.S. economy appears to allow people a greater degree of choice than ever before about how hard they want to work. The reality, though, is that if you want to have a successful career, you had better be prepared to be flexible about the number of hours you are willing to dedicate to your job. Right now, the flexibility goes only one way: toward more hours of work. In the current environment, an unwillingness to work long hours now might well result in being laid off. In that sense, the choice to work long hours is not really a choice at all.

As I noted earlier, the balance of power today strongly favors employers, at least temporarily. No matter where we are in the economic cycle, however, the New Normal demands that you be flexible about which hours you work. The successful formula for people is the same as for businesses: those who are most flexible will win.

It's not just that there is more work to do, but also more kinds of work for each person. The corporate fixation with productivity has given employees more responsibility and thus more stress. Keeping a reasonable work-work balance is hard enough. Work-life balance is even harder, at least until the 2001–2002 recession is a distant memory.

WORKING LONGER IN SECRET

It hasn't always been this way. In the decades following World War II—the era of big institutions and big bureaucracy—conformity was the order of the day, and working long hours was frowned upon in our society. Both blue-collar and white-collar workers got home in time for a family dinner. If you worked in a blue-collar trade, you might have avoided working harder or longer hours because it would have reflected poorly on peers, who were bound to take notice and offense.

In white-collar environments, there was a view that those who couldn't finish their work by 6:00 p.m. were disorganized, inefficient, and/or incompetent. There were a few obvious exceptions—accountants at tax season, lawyers preparing for a trial, doctors performing emergency surgery—but these professions had compensating time off. There was even a time when doctors routinely played golf on Wednesday afternoons.

If you were the kind of person who wanted to work harder than your peers, you did so in private. If possible, the goal was to create the impression that success came to you effortlessly, not through hard work. If you don't believe me, just watch how white-collar workers are represented in movies from the 1940s and 1950s.

My father-in-law was a remarkable—and wonderful—man. A retired police sergeant, he was proud of me, despite our fundamentally different views of work. But he sought to protect me from myself. If he found me working in his house, he would always say, "Don't kill the job!" He always said it with a smile. His view was that work was important, but it should never be allowed to interfere with family life. He worried that I worked to excess. We talked about this issue frequently, and I think he came to appreciate that while I liked my work, I viewed it as a way to ensure a better family life. His daughter shared my view, and my father-in-law came to appreciate that the two of us had a made a choice with which we were very happy.

You may conclude that I'm a workaholic, but then how do you explain the band? Or this book? Or the other stuff I do? When I work, I throw myself into it. It's really important to me to excel at my work. The same is true with my music. It drives me crazy when I don't play really well.

If you want to be professionally successful in the New Normal, you have to throw yourself into your work, but I don't think work for its own sake is the way to go. If we accept the notion that your career is a marathon, then you need nourishment along the way. Nourishment comes from having a life: family, hobbies, charities, a band. Whatever works for you. What matters is that you be passionate about your work and your life.

INVESTOR ALERT

Throughout this book, I emphasize the importance of working hard in the New Normal. One of the really surprising things about Wall Street is that hard work can help you succeed, but it's no guarantee. As in most aspects of life, luck really matters on Wall Street. So does good decision making. Lucky people who work hard and make good decisions almost always get very rich. So next time you buy a stock, remember that you are competing with lots of people who work very hard to understand that stock, a few people who are exceptionally gifted decision makers, a few others who are really lucky, and a very small number of people who have all three factors going for them. If none of these factors describes you, you are at a significant disadvantage.

HOW 24/7 EVOLVED

When global competition picked up steam in the 1980s, the postwar view of the workday faced a moment of truth. In some countries—notably the United States and Great Britain—society chose "work hard–play hard." They took advantage of globalization and technology to recast their economies. They built new industries—personal computers and cellular phones are examples—from scratch while phasing out others. The benefits of this approach were huge, namely the longest and most powerful economic expansion of the postwar period. Meanwhile, the rest of the developed world was more reluctant to abandon old ways. That was a choice they made, and it had economic consequences.

The recent evolution of economics has seen production move from local to global. In the days when agriculture dominated the economy, goods were produced and consumed in close proximity. The calendar and clock of agriculture dominated economic life. At planting and harvest time, the days were exceptionally long. In winter, the workday was short. The industrial revolution saw big advances in productivity, the first widespread shipping of nonluxury goods, and the introduction of world time. It is no coincidence that time zones appeared at the same time as the railroads. The railroads required standardized time in order to operate on schedule . . . and to avoid accidents. Supported by the emerging technology of the telegraph, railroads enabled goods to be moved long distances over land. It was not until the late twentieth century, when intercontinental telephone and fax enabled rich, low-cost communication around the world, that globalization became a reality.

Globalization is economics without borders. Armed with my BlackBerry, I can receive e-mail and phone calls almost anywhere in the world. As long as the BlackBerry is on, it works. It's pretty amazing. With tools like that, production can take place wherever the balance of cost and capability dictate. The forces at work in the economy today have been building since the Arab oil embargo of 1973 to 1974. The embargo played a big role in intensifying global competition. Whereas American companies had been accustomed to having their way—to competing only with other American companies—they suddenly faced competition from Japan and Europe. Facing substantially higher energy costs, American companies large and small needed to become more efficient. Some companies could not adjust, and so they disappeared. The survivors learned to operate with a reduced headcount. Computers and telecommunications equipment allowed them to achieve previously unfathomable levels of efficiency—and to keep meticulous track of everybody's productivity. The consequence of these multiple trends? Longer hours started to become the norm.

I've already talked about the astonishing ease of global voice and fax communications. But they represent only two-thirds of the communications story. The Internet is the other third. The Internet has made it easy for engineers to collaborate in real time between Silicon Valley and Singapore—or asynchronously, which is often more important. It has enabled companies to manufacture goods in one place and sell globally. Investors can trade twenty-four hours a day, moving from market to market by following the sun. Large companies have call centers in multiple time zones to handle customer queries at any hour of the day or night. Thanks to computer and communications technology, the 24/7 workday is possible. For most, it's a love-hate relationship but it's here to stay. Take full advantage of it.

IT'S NOT A CHOICE

As I noted earlier, the good news is that anyone—from corporations to individuals—can participate in the global economy. The bad news is that doing so requires a more flexible view of working hours. If you want to do business with someone twelve time zones away, there will be times when you need to be available during that person's business hours.

The same innovations that make it possible for everybody to operate in a single global time zone also reduce the pain of doing so. One good thing about doing business across continents is that the pain cuts both ways. The people at both ends of the transaction have to be available. As a result, it's generally possible to establish protocols of communication that enable everyone involved to have a life, even if it's interrupted from time to time by work. Technology and globalization have changed the world's perception of work hours, blurring the distinctions between work and leisure. Whether you work for a large company or for yourself, the opportunity to work long hours is there. The only question is whether to answer the call. That is a decision you must make for yourself.

Here's how I think about it. I don't like to bet on long shots, so I try to choose the path with greater certainty. In the New Normal, that calls for embracing the inevitability of the 24/7 workweek. The trick is to make the best of it. I have spent years experimenting with different ideas about this.

First, I try to optimize my time as a whole rather than looking at work and family time as separate entities. My goal is to maximize the quality as well as the quantity of time under my control. To this end, I am always looking for ways to reduce the amount of my personal time that is spent on low-value activities, such as going to the bank, shopping, or cleaning the house.

TAKING CONTROL

Technology plays a role in helping me control my life, and controlling one's life is an essential element of the 24/7 culture. Whenever possible, I bank and shop online. TiVo allows me to watch the television shows I choose at the time that suits me best. These and other technologies have freed up time for more valuable activities.

Human services also make my life easier. Rather than spending days trying to debug new computer products, I pay a technology expert to do it for me in a fraction of the time. When I see a cool new product I want to purchase, the first thing I ask is, "What needs to be done to get this thing to work properly?"

I have an actual office with a desk and a phone, but I don't spend much time there. My response to the 24/7 culture is to have communications devices and a backpack with a mobile office that come with me wherever I happen to be. I carry all the tools I need to do my job. In a pinch, I can catch up on work when nothing else important is going on. I can work from a Starbucks or a mountain summit, but I only do that when I have to. There are still reasons to go to an office, but they are fewer in number every year.

My last and most important piece of advice about working in a 24/7 world: don't work longer just because there are things to do. There are always things to do. And there are always people who will take advantage of your willingness to work on their behalf. Work longer because doing so will make your life better in the long run. While you're at it, keep track of the ways that working harder is making your life better. Making your life better takes time, so be patient and be realistic. And work smart. But don't compromise. Time is the most precious thing you have. Guard it fiercely.

.15.

SMALL IS BIGGER AND BETTER

Small businesses rule.

Do you realize there are more than 24 million small businesses in the United States? That's one small business for every 12.1 people. As staggering as that figure seems, we're on the verge of a monsoon of new small businesses. They already represent more than 99 percent of all employers in America—that's not a typo—and create 80 percent of all new jobs. Now, the New Normal will fertilize more small businesses—and more successful small businesses—than at any time in recent memory.

What we have now is a perfect alignment of stars. The climate is ideal for starting new businesses at a time when more and more people are about to discover that entrepreneurship is their best option.

In the late 1990s people started businesses because they *thought* it was their best option. But there was too much capital supporting too many entrepreneurs who were motivated by the promise of a quick and lucrative exit strategy. People started businesses in order to win an easy jackpot. They started businesses with minimal upfront preparation and with little understanding of the industry they were getting into.

It's not surprising that so many start-ups failed. Entrepreneurs were operating with the same level of self-delusion that goes into a typical Lotto ticket purchase and investing about as much upfront planning as they would devote to a weekend at the beach. I was at ground zero for start-ups and can say with complete confidence that this is less of a broad, sweeping generalization than you might imagine.

So why, given the stunning failures and lower levels of funding, am I predicting a deluge of small businesses? There are many reasons. The benefits of working in large corporations—not to mention, the opportunities—are diminishing. In the past it was generally easier to work for a large enterprise than to start your own business. These days, working for a big company is a lot like working for a start-up, anyway—without the upside. In the New Normal, setting up a business isn't a lot riskier than working for a corporation. And many of the businesses that will be started in the New Normal won't require a lot of capital. For more people than ever, entrepreneurship is becoming the best choice available.

By requiring their employees to assume added responsibilities, lean corporations are effectively grooming a generation of entrepreneurs. Until relatively recently, jobs were so targeted that most people toiled as cogs in a big machine. As companies started laying off employees, the survivors' jobs got bigger and bigger. Suddenly, they could see their operation from different angles. They developed broader skill sets and became more valuable. And now that big companies aren't promising job security, a start-up begins to look like a viable alternative.

AN END TO THE SCALE ADVANTAGE

Large enterprises are hot for anything that helps them maintain flexibility. Bent on reducing fixed costs—especially rapidly growing health-care benefits—enterprises are looking to outsource many of the functions that historically have been performed in-house. Layoffs and restructuring have created an abundance of skilled people capable of forming companies to provide those goods and services. It is increasingly common to see a marketing manager or engineer form a venture to sell his service back to a former employer—and to others. In coming years, we'll see huge numbers of start-ups formed around functions outsourced by large companies.

Meanwhile, world markets are budding at a time when corporate and individual consumers are less interested than ever in one-size-fits-all products and services. It's relatively easy for highly focused small businesses to deliver customized solutions to micro-segments. And there is less friction for new businesses in the U.S. economic system than in any other in the world.

At the same time, technology is swiftly removing the scale advantage large companies have enjoyed for years. It also is making it far easier than ever to conduct the critical task of information gathering required to launch a successful business. And technology is providing new tools to help those start-ups operate efficiently.

Over the past decades, a parade of technological advances has cleared the path for anyone contemplating a business. Now new technology is catapulting those businesses forward: expanding the reach of small businesses and giving them new niches of opportunity that aren't dominated by the big guys. "On the Web you can take your abilities and magnify them," says Mark Vadon, the CEO of the online jewelry retailer Blue Nile.

Blue Nile now is generating more than $148 million in

revenues and has been profitable since 2002, making fools of critics who predicted that its business model—which involves leveraging the existing diamond-supply chain to sell engagement rings and gift jewelry to men over the Internet—was a doomed idea. Today, Blue Nile owns 2½ percent of the U.S. market for diamond engagement rings. When the company went public in May 2004, it became the first IPO in the retail sector since 2002 to be priced above its estimated offering range.

CALLING FOR LESS CAPITAL

Blue Nile was an unusual Internet mania success story. Most entrepreneurs who started companies at the same time as Blue Nile were not very smart about investing the capital that was flooding in. For many, the primary skill appeared to be in spending capital, not creating value. When the money ran out, hundreds of companies simply disappeared. The venture capital industry has licked its wounds and gotten back into the game, but it has done so with renewed caution. As a result, fewer deals receive funding, and the amount of capital per deal is low relative to what it was in the late 1990s.

The reduced availability of venture capital can actually be a positive thing for entrepreneurs. For the good ones, at least. Less capital means fewer bad businesses competing for management talent. (Or, in Silicon Valley parlance, it has "cleared out the riffraff.") The limited funding should also curb the number of me-too businesses competing for customers. With fewer investments per venture capitalist, entrepreneurs can count on more time—and help—from their investors.

One of the key questions that every entrepreneur should ask is, Is venture capital the right thing for my start-up? The odds are that it isn't. Venture firms fund only a small percentage of the start-ups in this country. Venture capitalists focus most of their effort in a limited number of industries: information technology, health-care technology, and, to a lesser extent, consumer services. It's relatively unusual for venture firms to stray from their areas of focus, so it's really important that you make sure that your plan is a good match for the firms you approach. You should also know that there is no point in sending your plan to people who do not know you. Venture capital is a people business. Firms are very busy just looking at deals sponsored by people they know. If you don't know any partners at a venture firm you want to approach, find someone who does and ask that person to make an introduction.

Keep in mind that the act of raising money is, in effect, a form of disclosure. Sure, you can plaster the word *Confidential* all over your business plan, but the reality is that the act of raising money will raise your profile in ways that will complicate your life if you are not prepared. You can limit the impact of this disclosure by getting your business out of the "idea" stage and into the "real company" stage prior to seeking venture capital.

There's another critical advantage. The more value you can add before taking a dollar from the outside, the more likely your business will succeed. And the greater your percentage ownership will be. Bill Gates didn't take any money until Microsoft had about $24 million in revenues. Venture firms did not want to invest when Intuit was a start-up, so founder Scott Cook didn't take any money until Intuit had about $30 million in revenues. Why did they take venture money so late? Bill Gates and Scott Cook were looking for business advisers and partners to help them make the most of their opportunities. In both cases, the decision was sound.

This is an enormously valuable thing to know: the best business plans don't require capital. The best businesses are those in which customers like the product or service so much that their purchases underwrite the cost of building the business. My favorite example is eBay, which was profitable from practically its first day of operation. A useful rule of thumb: there's an inverse correlation between the amount of capital required and the attractiveness of the business plan.

INVESTOR ALERT

Next time you look at a rapidly growing public company—or an initial public offering (IPO)—look closely at the "paid in capital" line in the balance sheet and compare it to the profit margin. How much capital did it take before the company turned profitable? How long did it take? There are no hard and fast rules about how much capital and time it should take to achieve profitability, but in both cases, less is better. Time and capital intensity are bad for investors, so you need to be vigilant. On time and capital alone, biotechnology stands out as a tough investment proposition. And that's before the staggering uncertainties associated with drug development. A new category that demands a similarly cautious approach is nanotechnology, an industry that is so far from maturity that it may be years before the first commercial products come to market.

LARGE FOOTPRINTS FOR SMALL OPERATIONS

As Blue Nile founder Vadon discovered, any start-up can deploy Web technology. He also learned that the Internet allows any company to project whatever image it wants, regardless of size. Even as a start-up, Blue Nile competed successfully with Tiffany in that legendary company's core business. Blue Nile taught men how to buy diamonds, and it provided a wider selection of gems than Tiffany. By leveraging the Interent, Blue Nile was able to offer much lower prices. No wonder the company is successful.

If you go to eBay, you will see an entire marketplace based on the small operation–large footprint phenomenon. Vendors have set up shop to sell everything from software overstocks to juice extractors to motorcycles. Every vendor looks pretty much the same. eBay is about the products and the community. With good products and prices, and good customer service, even a one-person firm can be a big success on eBay.

The people at eBay have made it relatively painless to become an online retailer, providing all the necessary tools and cross-promotion to sell products to customers anywhere in the world. It's not the same thing as having storefronts in every major city around the globe, but it's a whole lot cheaper and easier to manage. eBay isn't the right marketplace for every product, but for start-up retail businesses, it's one of the really good places to start.

On eBay you can test your ideas and learn your market with relatively low risk. The next notch up in sophistication would be your own Web site, selling direct through your own Internet storefront, shipping to customers globally via FedEx or UPS. This too, is easier than ever. Thanks to Overture and Google, you can use pay-for-performance advertising to bring customers to your site.

Just as global access is no longer restricted to large companies, the declining cost of technology—and expanding functionality—means small companies now can afford the same technology innovations that have helped large enterprises operate effectively. Ironically, it's generally easier to implement those technologies in small companies. Wireless data devices such as Research in Motion's BlackBerry, Handspring's Treo, and Danger's Sidekick are affordable and widely available. Microsoft offers small-business configurations of its suite of Web services technology. Intuit has fabulous products for small-business accounting, tax preparation, and payroll. If you prefer to buy these capabilities as a service, H&R Block, Paychex, and others stand ready to serve you.

According to InStat, small businesses spent $161 billion on information technology in 2003, a year when about 70 percent of small businesses lacked a Web site. The economics of the Web are so attractive that many more small businesses will establish an Internet presence in the decade to come. What's more, I suspect that one of the most compelling areas for start-ups in the years ahead will be new products and services to help small businesses succeed.

In the New Normal, you can outsource practically anything to get your business started. Now that I'm in my third start-up, I believe I have outsourced just about everything possible in the investment business. The choice is up to you. You can outsource reception and facilities management by starting out in an office with shared infrastructure. You can outsource back-office tasks such as accounting, payroll, benefits, and information technology. You can outsource manufacturing and fulfillment. The list goes on and on. What you cannot outsource is the value added of your business. Whatever that value added is has to be valuable enough to support the business as a whole. In my businesses, that value added comes from money management, not running an office. So we outsource as many office functions as possible. As my partner John Powell would often say, "Our job is to manage money, not people."

Today, there's even a trend among start-ups to outsource the administrative assistant role. Increasingly, the heavy paperwork burden inherent in any business is being tackled with the help of Virtual Assistants, the growing pool of remote office workers for hire. They typically charge twenty-five to thirty-five dollars per hour to write letters, maintain databases, coordinate schedules, transcribe meeting notes, complete documents, prepare presentations, contact business partners, or anything else required of a small business—when there's no need for a full-time on-site worker. Often, it's a purely online relationship: the assistants could be working in another time zone, and you might never meet face-to-face. An extreme example of this model can be found in the outsourcing market for Powerpoint presentations. There are companies in India that can produce a presentation in as few as three hours . . . at very reasonable prices. If you are artistically or temporally challenged, this kind of service is a godsend.

BLOCKING AND TACKLING BASICS

The environment for start-ups changes continuously, but the most important aspects of the start-up world are more or less permanent. The key to success is to understand the absolute truths of the start-up business, then make appropriate additions in keeping with the times.

Here's a simple example. Say you decide to get into the pink shirt business. For the purposes of this example, let's assume that you know nothing except that, in today's environment, people want pink shirts. That's a cool insight, but if that's all you know, you're bound to fail. If you want to be successful in *any* form of the shirt business, you have to know the shirt business itself. That's the core competence that will enable your business to succeed. If you're the best in the shirt business, succeeding in pink shirts will be a no-brainer. If you're not very good at making or selling shirts, the insight about pink shirts won't be worth much.

Whenever you make a financial commitment, timing really matters, but it's only one of many things you have to get right. Too many people start businesses focused on the temporal aspects, without understanding the absolute truths of business. Whenever I talk to entrepreneurs, I always focus on blocking and tackling basics. It's really sad how many entrepreneurs don't know the fundamentals.

Here's what I mean.

When people ask me what kind of business they should start, I tell them to start a business they really understand and love. Unless you are creating an industry from scratch, you will be competing with people who are already in the business you have targeted, people who do nothing else. If you start a business in an area you don't understand, the people who *do* understand the business are going to kick your butt. The high-percentage play is to start a business in the field in which you are already working. If that doesn't feel right to you, or if that's not possible, then you have lots of homework to do before you launch your start-up.

My friend Michael Blesius is deep in the homework stage of starting his own company. A former video technician for the NBC-TV affiliate in San Jose, Michael saw a limited future in his profession. Hence, he decided to pursue a business involving his passion: coffee. He went to visit an old friend who owned a coffee shop where Michael had worked ten years earlier. He remembered it as "the best job of my life." The woman who owned the shop was thinking of selling, and Michael was thinking of buying. He asked me for advice, and I suggested he do some research on the business. I outlined a few ideas for his research, knowing that the first homework assignment would provide a real indication of Michael's enthusiasm and commitment to entrepreneurship.

Two weeks later Michael strode into my office with a binder full of material. He had copies of the owner's sales reports—which she had supplied—as well as a map he created indicating every coffee shop within a ten-mile radius. He had data on traffic patterns. He had carefully drawn layouts of every coffee shop in the area. He brought in menus for each competitor, as well as surveys he had conducted of what customers bought in each shop. He had clearly spent every minute of the two weeks on this project. His work was brilliant.

It was clear that Michael possessed the drive to pursue his dream. But the research binder also revealed two other things. First, that the coffee shop Michael was considering, at the price being asked, lacked promise. Even if Michael did a great job, he would not make enough money to justify his effort, much less the investment he would have to make. Second, despite his enthusiasm and dedication, Michael lacked the experience needed to run a successful coffee shop. I suggested he learn all he could about the business. To accomplish that, I suggested he work at a successful coffee shop or enter the training program at Starbuck's or Peet's Coffee and Teas.

About a week later he phoned to say that he had taken an entry-level job as a barrista at Peet's, the San Francisco Bay Area's preeminent coffee operation. Some people would not have taken an entry-level job, viewing it as a big comedown. Those people are not my kind of entrepreneur. True entrepreneurs do whatever it takes to succeed. It took no time before Michael was promoted. Now he's scheduled for another promotion. By the time Michael finds the perfect coffee shop to buy, he'll know as much about the business as anyone. I'll bet he winds up with a chain of awesome coffee shops.

That's how it's done.

One of the basic and most important rules when you're starting a business is to truly understand what it is you're doing. In any economic endeavor, the statistics favor the most prepared person. Forget what the pundits tell you to do. Pundits make lousy entrepreneurs. The key thing is to know your subject matter. Know it better than your competitors. When I'm considering backing an entrepreneur, I'm interested in someone who genuinely understands the market he or she is going after, and has a tremendous command of the data. I'm always impressed with people who have on the tip of their tongue the exact metrics that make a difference in their business.

WHERE OPPORTUNITY LIVES

If you're looking for opportunities, the first thing to do is ask yourself if there are aspects of your current job that can stand on their own. If the thing you know well can be a stand-alone business, you are off to a great start. If it can't, think about what you like to do and are good at doing.

Need ideas? Here's a big one: personal services. What do people always seem to be lacking? Time. No one has enough of it. People are prepared to pay a lot of money to save time. And everyone's needs are different. As a result, there is an endless demand for new start-ups to provide personal services. The best thing about personal-services businesses is that you don't have to be first. You just have to be good.

Take the business founded by another friend of mine, Harley Brookins. A former flight attendant, Harley started a business of driving people to the airport in their own car. This model allowed him to start without any capital, and it also allowed him to price his service to compete with the short-term parking rates at San Francisco International Airport. One day he realized he could get his customers' cars serviced while they were out of town. Next, he was taking their packages to FedEx, buying gifts, taking Grandma to the beauty salon. Next thing I knew, Harley's business had blossomed into a ten-employee operation. He owns a fleet of cars and has become incredibly successful. He performs little miracles for people who don't have enough time. He's so good, I wrote a song about him.

In the United States, people gain a big part of their identity—and self-worth—from work. Statistics indicate that Americans work more hours than people in the countries that are our major trading partners. Americans trade time for money, but not because they don't value time. Time—or rather, the lack of it—creates a market opportunity that is limited only by imagination. Maybe it's a service. But perhaps it's a product. It will be whatever you make it.

What are you good at? Who do you know? What will customers pay for to gain more time? Opportunity sits at the intersection of the answers to those three questions. If you're an inventor, invent something that gives people more time. If you're a programmer, design software that gives people more time. If you are a master chef, give them better-tasting food that takes less time.

The range of small-business opportunities today is extremely wide. In addition to personal services or time-saving innovations, offering customers unique solutions to time-consuming tasks also provides a wide opening. Big companies are generally best positioned for the mass customization elements of demand but not necessarily the highly customized or niche portions. And as the economy moves away from a mass-market orientation, more and more customers demand flexible solutions or custom-fit goods. These can exist in almost every sector of the economy. The trick for all entrepreneurs is to know their customers and deliver products or services that those customers value.

The automobile industry was one of the first to migrate from mass market to mass customization. You may recall the words of Henry Ford, who said that customers could have a Model T in any color they wanted, "as long as it is black." That is the epitome of mass market. Everyone got exactly the same thing. Eventually, car companies figured out that they could sell more cars at higher average prices if they offered a mix of options, including paint color. More recently, smaller businesses have emerged to do custom van conversions, custom paint jobs, and the like. The key to success for these small businesses is a customer base willing to pay for a vendor's value added. This is the secret of microbreweries, specialty medical practices, and marketing-services firms.

WHY PLANNING MATTERS

I have started three businesses during my career. I have invested in dozens of start-ups. Along the way, I have learned a few things about what makes a start-up successful. The first of these is obvious, but often overlooked: you should do everything in your power to make your start-up successful.

Planning and analysis at the front end is the best way to eliminate pain later on. If there is a flaw in your idea, the best time to discover it is during the planning stage, when it is easy and inexpensive to make changes . . . or to start over. Business failures are costly, and it often takes years to clean up the mess. Just remember that time is the most precious thing you have.

I'm a big believer in formal business plans. Many people think a business plan is a document that you give to potential investors. That's only half the story. The first priority of a business plan is to help you organize your business and make it successful. If it's good enough to make the business work, it will generally be good enough to help you raise money. Think of the business plan as a recipe for the business. It includes both a list of ingredients for the venture and the steps for making those ingredients into a successful business. Intellectual honesty is essential to the planning process. If you don't identify the critical success factors—and the issues to be addressed—up front, they will come back to haunt you later on. The goal is to understand the critical success factors and gather all the resources necessary to make success happen.

If you don't have a good business plan before you start, your chances of success are greatly reduced. Many entrepreneurs don't create business plans because they are too busy. Others avoid detailed business planning because it is difficult. Still others think that developing a business plan is boring. My experience is that enthusiasm for business planning is a leading indicator of future success among entrepreneurs. Think about the story of Michael Blesius. If you don't have time for a plan or don't feel like doing one, the risk of failure rises dramatically. Ask yourself this question: How would I feel if my start-up were to fail? You should ask that question because failure can happen even to start-ups that are well planned and well funded. But it happens far more often to those that are not well planned and well funded.

The people who think business plans are only useful for raising money sometimes think it's beneficial to inflate all the projections. That is a mistake. In making forecasts, make reasonable assumptions and apply them consistently. Investors will not accept your projections at face value. They will want to know how you plan to achieve your projections. If your business plan doesn't stand up to scrutiny, you won't be able to raise money.

A great business plan honestly identifies the risks and describes the venture's strategy for minimizing them. It identifies competitors, as well as their strengths and weaknesses. When someone tells me their start-up has no competitors, my assumption is that they have not done their homework. The more complete and accurate the business plan, the more effective it will be as a planning tool and the more effective it will be as a fund-raising tool.

INVESTOR ALERT

Whenever I research a stock, I pay particular attention to competitors. I compile a list of actual and potential threats, recognizing that markets can and do change. Most often, competition comes down to scale and business model. All else being equal, the bigger company usually wins. However, it is rare that all else is equal. In that case, new business models can offset the advantages of scale. This is how upstarts displace market leaders. It is how Dell overtook Compaq and how Wal-Mart overtook Sears. Why do large companies allow this to happen? Successful companies tend to fall in love with their business model and do not evolve with their market. In extreme cases—Eastman Kodak's failure to anticipate digital photography is an example—the damage may be irreversible.

GETTING FROM FEAR TO GREED

Investors face a constant battle between fear and greed. My recommendation is that you should first focus on eliminating fear. My partner John Powell and I learned this lesson when we were trying to persuade John Doerr and his venture capital partners at Kleiner Perkins Caufield & Byers (KPCB) to back our start-up, Integral Capital Partners, in 1991. Not only was Integral a new concept—a crossover fund that involved both later-stage venture and public market investing—but we were also proposing to be a KPCB affiliate. This risk to KPCB was more than financial. Backing Integral also entailed franchise risk, as a failure by us would damage KPCB's reputation.

It is quite understandable that Doerr and his partners would be very cautious about taking on the double risk entailed by our plan. John Powell and I had to allay their concerns. Among the fears: they didn't understand how we could manage the asset level we proposed with only two people. So John and I produced time-and-motion studies—based on our real-life experience at T. Rowe Price Associates—to show them how it would work. We had done this before, but there was no reason for KPCB to take our word for it. So we analyzed our calendar for the prior year. We created a chart showing how our time would be spent. The evidence did not just make KPCB more comfortable with our plan. It also alleviated our own fears.

When you are building a business plan, your first priority should be to eliminate investor—and your own—concerns about the downside. Demonstrate your mastery of the business opportunity. Demonstrate your plans for dealing with challenges and competition. Demonstrate command of key business metrics. If you do this, potential investors' fears will diminish. At that point, they can get excited about the potential upside. That's when greed takes over.

If you are considering venture capital funding, there are a few other rules of thumb that you should keep in mind.

First, remember that funding from venture firms is very expensive. If your company is a raw start-up, the investors may ask for half or more of your company in exchange for an investment of a few million dollars. My advice is to move your business plan forward as far as possible before seeking venture capital. The more market research, analysis of competitors, product development, business planning, and team development you can do before pitching venture investors, the higher the probability that someone will invest and the more favorable the deal you will cut.

Second, venture firms get most excited about big ideas, those that have a realistic opportunity to reach $100 million in revenue within five or six years. Not surprisingly, their favorite deals are big ideas that require little effort or capital on their part. The secret of the venture capital business is to leverage the work of many smart and hardworking entrepreneurs simultaneously. If this doesn't sound fair to you, welcome to the world of entrepreneurship.

Third, venture firms get most excited about start-ups that offer better, faster, cheaper solutions in large existing markets rather than those that aim to create brand-new markets. The latter generally require too much capital and entail greater risk. Why, you might ask, are venture capitalists funding biotechnology firms, which often require hundreds of millions in funding to reach profitability? I'm still trying to figure that one out.

As I mentioned earlier, the more capital a venture requires, the greater the risk. The best ideas are the ones that don't require any capital at all. Again, eBay is a great example. eBay founder Pierre Omidyar coded the first version of eBay in his spare time. He put it up on the Web and people started using it right away. EBay began life as an online flea market where sellers paid a small fee to sell their merchandise. The business was profitable from the beginning. When Omidyar brought in venture capital from Benchmark Capital, it was to get a smart partner to help him optimize eBay's strategy and execution. He didn't need the capital.

EBay illustrates my "growing pie theory of entrepreneurship." The first instinct of many people is to maximize their share of the pie as represented by ownership percentage. My philosophy is to focus on maximizing the size of the pie. I'm not suggesting you give away pieces of your business willy-nilly, but rather that you should trade shares of your business to gather the ingredients necessary for success. If you are smart about it, you can use equity in your company to get everything you need to be successful. Owning 10 percent of a big success can be far more valuable than 100 percent ownership of a moderate success, and infinitely more valuable than 100 percent of a failure.

EXECUTING IDEAS

Entrepreneurship depends on good ideas, but execution of those ideas is what determines success or failure. Consider the restaurant business. Many entrepreneurs start restaurants because they like their own cooking. Good cooking is essential, but it's only one factor necessary to success. Successful restaurants understand their cost structure at the per-meal-served level, have a marketing strategy to draw customers, are good people managers, and have enough capital to give the business plan time to succeed. And they don't try to create a restaurant chain until they have the first restaurant running perfectly.

My friend Harley didn't have a business plan that called for deploying a staff of ten drivers and a fleet of cars. He started with no cars—he drove customers in their own car—and focused his energy on customer service. He built his business organically. One satisfied customer led to another. Then it was a simple matter of adding drivers and cars. The best way to build a business is to start small. Get the business model right. Get the details right. Then replicate.

Just as you need to understand the essence of what you're doing you also need to understand what a dollar of input here does in terms of a dollar of output there. Cisco Systems didn't know how big the market for routers was going to be, but they understood that customers would pay high prices, enabling the company to make high profits even at a relatively low sales level. The founders demonstrated to the venture capitalists at Sequoia Capital that the market could support that level of sales. Once Cisco executed that plan, new ideas for growth were everywhere. It added a new feature here and a new product there. After a few years, Cisco was the hottest company in the data networking business. Most successful companies are like that.

One of the most common mistakes during the Internet mania was the perception that a great idea was all you needed to be successful. I actually think ideas are less important than execution. Face it. A lot of people who start small businesses avoid conducting thorough market research because it takes time and hard work. And, of course, they would run the risk of being told that their idea is a loser. If you want to be successful, you have to seek out feedback from people who matter, even if their feedback is negative. I'd rather get the bad news early. Take the time to solicit feedback from people you trust. Lots of them. You can even give them an incentive to be helpful to you.

I believe really strongly that most great ideas will happen.

As tempting as it is to think that venture capitalists act as judge and jury over ideas, the fact is that customers act as judge and jury. When a good idea doesn't work, the problem may be related to execution . . . or timing. There are a huge number of ideas that come to market before their time. Apple's Newton is a good example. No amount of promotional activity, no amount of research and development was going to make that "personal digital assistant" into a great product. It was too big, too expensive, and it didn't do enough. A decade later, Research in Motion's BlackBerry is the market leader in personal digital assistants. It's perfectly sized, appropriately priced, and delivers great value.

In contrast to the Newton, Apple's iPod came to market with perfect timing. It seemingly came out of nowhere. Apple had the brilliant insight that customers would pay a premium to put a thousand songs in their pocket. The company bundled it with a great piece of software that took all the pain out of making music portable. Apple got all the pieces right because they analyzed every aspect of the opportunity, assembled everything that was needed to exploit it—and the timing was right.

Start-ups are not easy, so it's important that you really love the business you choose. My rule of thumb is this: If you can't imagine doing anything else, do your start-up. If you can imagine something else, do that instead.

THE TOOLS KEEP ROLLING IN

For all the challenges inherent in starting your own company, the tools for doing so are better than ever. It is worth noting that tools for small businesses have typically come from small businesses, some of which are pretty big now. Look at the success of Salesforce.com.

Founded in 1999 by former Oracle executive Marc Benioff, Salesforce.com sells tools for salespeople as an online service accessible via a Web browser. Historically, software aimed at sales force automation (SFA) and customer relationship management (CRM) has been both expensive and hard to deploy. Because its product is hosted online, Salesforce.com provides the benefits of SFA and CRM without the need for high-priced software and the IT infrastructure to deploy and support it. If your small business does any kind of direct sales, you should check out Salesforce.com.

With a business model that takes advantage of the declining costs of computer technology and bandwidth, Salesforce.com easily encroached on territory controlled by traditional industry leader Siebel—which built its business on multi-million-dollar software packages that sometimes took a year or more to install. Salesforce.com only began to offer its on-demand SFA application service in February 2000. By January 31, 2003, it generated revenues of $50.9 million. It has turned a profit every quarter since April 2003, and raised $110 million in its June 2004 IPO.

And then there's BlueTie, one of the many private companies offering small businesses e-mail, calendar, contacts, and messaging applications via a hosted Web-based subscription service. Founded in 1999 by CEO David Koretz when he was a mere teen, BlueTie provides Microsoft Outlook–like functionality for small businesses who want to upgrade from free Yahoo! or Hotmail e-mail accounts but also want to avoid the significant up-front and ongoing cost of Outlook, which requires the purchase and support of a server, Microsoft Exchange Server software, and Outlook.

Koretz can thank two important developments for his business' early success: broadband's growing penetration and Microsoft's unwillingness to cannibalize its own server software business by offering a similar service. (This is another example of the business model inflexibility that I mentioned in the preceding Investor Alert.) With revenues of $1 million in 2002, Koretz says that sales rose by 1,200 percent in 2003, and that BlueTie ended the year with positive cash flow. BlueTie still faces an uphill battle because the announcement of a competing service from Microsoft would be life threatening, even if BlueTie had sales of $100 million.

Like many trends, the emergence of small businesses that deliver tools to other small businesses has been brewing for years. In the 1920s, former U.S. Army pilot Sherman C. Amsden had trouble reaching his doctor during a family medical emergency. Motivated by the inconvenience, Amsden started Telanswerphone, one of the first telephone-answering companies. By 1950, Amsden wanted to take the concept one step farther. He collaborated with inventor Richard Florac to introduce the first commercial pager. The new company, Aircall Inc., counted among its initial customers doctors, salesmen, detectives, plumbers, and undertakers.

What Amsden really gave the world was mobility. Today mobility is central to our economy and culture. A wide range of electronic devices ensure that anyone—including entrepreneurs—can keep a business running smoothly from afar.

In 1992, Silicon Valley start-up Intuit introduced QuickBooks, accounting software so easy to use that small business owners could dispense with the need for a professional bookkeeper. With a user interface modeled on a checkbook, QuickBooks has liberated a generation of entrepreneurs from the tyranny of double-entry accounting. It's not just that QuickBooks saves time, it lowers the cost of running a small business.

QuickBooks became the market leader for business accounting software exactly one month after it was launched. Lurking behind that success is an amazing irony. For three years, Intuit routinely overlooked customer survey data indicating that as many as 48 percent of the users of its Quicken home-finance software were using it for business, as well as personal accounting. "We ignored it because our mindset was that we had built a consumer product," recalled co-founder Scott Cook. Ultimately, the company pursued the small-business market with QuickBooks, outselling the competition by a two-to-one margin in the first month. "If a surprise happens, and most people in business don't want to admit to surprises, it's the market speaking to you. It's telling you that there's an opportunity you never saw," said Cook.

Okay, so it's 2004 and entrepreneurs are looking to build a next generation of tools for small businesses, using the Internet as a foundation. Half a dozen start-ups are selling services designed to enable entrepreneurs to expand their network of business contacts without ever having to shake a hand or attend a trade show. Known as social networking companies, they use the Internet to leverage the concept of six degrees of separation. Every entrepreneur struggles to get to the right people at the right time. What they need is a search engine for business or social contacts they can trust.

In one variation, companies like Friendster, LinkedIn, and Ryze search among their members for friends of friends who can help you. At Ryze, members keen on establishing business contacts build a page about themselves, listing their haves and wants. Or, if you go with Visible Path, you can build a business network within your company that facilitates relationship-based contacts in a way that protects the privacy of the contactee. The software identifies interpersonal connections from e-mail, phone, and other communications media and constructs a map of relationships. When a person inside the company wants to exploit a relationship, he or she consults the map and makes a request to the one or more people who have the relationship or are on the path to it. The system protects "contactees" by giving them the power to accept or decline requests for contacts on an anonymous basis. And because Visible Path is an enterprise product, it can provide security with respect to the contacts, e-mail, and phone calls it screens for the database.

For any business-networking service to work, the contactee must get some benefit. The risk is that some contactees might view the social network as a form of spam. The social network concept depends on the enthusiastic participation of a relatively small number of people with great relationships.

The snag with this model is that the most valuable members are going to get far more attention than they want. If a clever entrepreneur can launch a service that gets past this issue, he or she may get very rich indeed. The challenge is to deliver enough value to enough users to build critical mass. It's too early to know which, if any, of the social-networking companies will succeed, but it is worth tracking their progress.

FINDING WHAT'S MISSING

Finally, small companies must be willing to be different. When Google started up in 1999, everyone in Silicon Valley *knew* you couldn't make money with a search engine. The leading search vendors of 1997, including Yahoo!, Excite, and Lycos, had migrated to a portal business model, hoping to offset the low value of page view advertising with massive scale. But Google—like Overture—saw the popularity of search as a potential platform for pay-for-performance advertising.

I discussed this need to be different with Intuit's Scott Cook. "It's not just being different, it's finding something fundamentally true that everyone else has missed and then incrementing your way to make it work," he said. "The biggest successes tend to be those that are not believed by others. Steve Jobs took the idea for Apple to his contract employer, Atari. Amazon was ridiculed. eBay was widely thought to be beneath comment. I'm sure if you pitched me the eBay idea, I wouldn't have gotten it. FedEx wasn't thought to be a big idea. The biggest opportunities tend to be those that everybody else has missed. They tend to represent a large mindset change and are generally not obvious to people with conventional wisdom, even after you tell them."

It worked for him.

If the idea and execution are good, small businesses do not remain small for long. I remember clearly when Microsoft was a very small company in the software business. I remember when Dell was an upstart. I remember when Amazon.com, Yahoo!, and Google were formed. But your start-up doesn't need to join the Fortune 500 to be a success. Many businesses—service businesses, in particular—can prosper without ever getting huge. The good news for successful entrepreneurs, though, is that the things that are so hard in the early days eventually become a lot easier. Plus, there is no business experience on Earth as satisfying as contributing to the success of a start-up.

.16.

THERE'S NEW LIFE AT THE TOP

It's always been lonely at the top. In the New Normal, it can be excruciatingly so. Throughout the decades, chief executive officers routinely faced challenges that would overwhelm lesser beings. But in the Old Normal, when the rules were fairly straightforward, the CEO who didn't know how to deal with a particular corner-office challenge could fall back on a trusty routine. He or she could close the door, take a deep breath, and calmly ask himself, "What would Jack Welch do?"

The New Normal is not particularly CEO-friendly. The same explosion of globalization, technology, and regulation that is creating so much uncertainty for everyone else is also a monumental headache for CEOs. There is no place for a CEO to take cover. The business world has been turned on its head, and nothing is as it was. Business processes passed down from generation to generation are under assault amid a transformation in supply chains and distribution. Shareholders are as impatient as ever, and feisty to boot.

Think of the new pressures facing CEOs today. Every CEO knows the game is different, but no one knows for sure what to do about it. Customers want it yesterday . . . at half the price. Global competitors are more formidable than ever. The new law that reforms corporate governance, the Sarbanes-Oxley Act of 2002, makes everything associated with corporate governance more expensive and complicated. The goal of Sarbanes-Oxley is to increase the independence of boards of directors so that they will act in the interests of shareholders more often than was the case in the late 1990s. But nobody has been through this before, so everything takes longer. Meanwhile, investors are demanding big-time results in an unbelievably short time frame. It was much simpler when you could be a tyrant and ignore everybody around you, back when CEOs could follow that timeworn path of their predecessors and peers: inaction.

POWERING THROUGH THE CONFUSION

From the CEO's perspective, there is some comfort in knowing that the New Normal is new for everyone. No company got a head start. No company can sit still. As much as it would be nice to be the CEO of Microsoft or Wal-Mart, even they have huge challenges. For those two companies, the penalty for more than two decades of innovation and customer satisfaction is an endless battle with politicians and regulators eager to flex muscles on a global scale. Most CEOs can count their blessings that they only have to contend with never-ending changes in the competitive landscape.

In typical New Normal fashion, though, there is a silver lining. Opportunity lurks around every corner for CEOs who are prepared to seize the moment. The trick is to get ahead of the curve on the two overarching business issues that require the attention of every CEO: globalization and technology. With respect to these two issues at least, inaction is not an option. CEOs who want to remain employed must find a way to power through the confusion and do the right thing. Technology is an incredible tool for business, but only for the people who make an effort to leverage it. You can't win if you don't play. If you do nothing, the outcome is bound to be bad.

If you are wondering where to start, consider your approach to management. How much has it changed in the past few years? If it hasn't changed a lot, start there. We are early in a new era that is challenging the orthodoxy of management. It used to be that size was a form of security in business. No longer. In the communications equipment industry, both Nortel and Lucent are much bigger than Juniper Networks, but they have been caught with the wrong business model, while Juniper has the right products and the right business model at the right time. But even companies like Juniper that are well positioned for the moment have to be vigilant. If things are going well for your company, do not relax. This is the New Normal. Any business that has not already been turned on its head soon will be.

MAKING GLOBALIZATION WORK FOR YOUR COMPANY

Globalization has changed the nature of business. It has forced every company to reconsider its mission, business processes, and opportunities. Whatever your company's addressable market was before, it's different today. It's probably larger, but not necessarily. Whatever your supply chain has been, there is probably a better one available.

Whoever your competitors were before, there are almost certainly more of them today. And whatever works for you today will probably need to change tomorrow. And the next day. And the day after that.

Globalization is dynamic in the extreme. In many ways, it is like a landscape of seaside dunes shifting constantly with the wind and tide. Today, China and India are where the action is, but only a few years ago, Southeast Asia and Mexico were the focus. In a few years, some new geography may command our attention. What matters is not which country is hot today but rather that no country—not even the United States—can sustain an upper hand without constant adaptation. In the globalization game, any country can play, and most do. For corporations, the only real choice is to participate. And the only way to participate is to experiment, evaluate, improve, evaluate some more, and improve again.

Every industry—and every company within an industry—should have its own approach to globalization. A strategy that works really well for a company you read about may not work so well for your company. For example, pundits are preaching the benefits of moving software development and call centers to India. The labor-cost advantages in India are obvious, but labor cost is only one of many important factors to be considered in software development and call centers.

When it comes to call centers, there are situations where India's cost advantage is compelling, and others where it falls short. One challenge of call centers in India is employee turnover, which is hardly surprising considering that everyone has to work the night shift. High turnover is a nonstarter for call centers that handle customer support for complex products. In software development, there are similar pitfalls to consider. If you are CEO of a start-up, for example, I wouldn't recommend that you move the development of your first product to the building next door, much less to a country halfway around the world. Product development—particularly in start-ups—is incredibly dynamic and requires continuous face-to-face collaboration. E-mail, phones, and even video conferencing are poor substitutes for a shared cubicle.

When it comes to outsourcing overseas, larger companies have more degrees of freedom than start-ups. Large companies have the operational scale that permits experimentation. They also have a greater incentive to optimize unit costs. But no company—large or small—can afford to make huge mistakes. You can protect yourself by experimenting. See what works before you move aggressively. Make sure you evaluate the effectiveness of each outsourced business process as a whole, not just the unit cost.

Smart CEOs have responded to globalization with strategies based on flexibility. In China, Coca-Cola sells more tea than cola. When change is the only certainty, flexibility is the best defense. Whatever worked yesterday may not work today, so keep looking for business processes to refine. As you study your customers, suppliers, and competitors, ask yourself what economic benefits you can derive from change. Flexibility has a cost—unit economics may not match up to traditional high-fixed-cost models—but the benefits may exceed the cost. And it may threaten constituencies within your company whose livelihood depends on maintaining the status quo. In any event, both the costs and benefits are subject to analysis, which is the necessary prelude to action.

To illustrate one company's recognition of the importance of flexibility, let me return to the example of Microsoft's outsourced manufacturing for its XBox video game console. At the end of 2002, Microsoft's supplier Flextronics was manufacturing all XBoxes in China. Then SARS broke out. For a period of months, Microsoft prohibited its employees from traveling to China. Suddenly, the unit-cost savings associated with manufacturing in China looked less attractive. What if supplies were disrupted by SARS? What if Microsoft employees became infected? Flextronics had the capability to manufacture XBoxes in North America and Europe, giving Microsoft tremendous flexibility. In the end, Microsoft did not shift XBox manufacturing, but it could have. And it still can.

As frustrating as it is to watch jobs migrate overseas, the end result is positive for the U.S. economy. Globalization has enabled formerly weak economies such as India and China to gain strength. Rising standards of living promote peace in the world's two most populous countries. The same thing has happened in Mexico and Brazil. Just as important, rising standards of living in these countries also create demand for American goods and services.

INVESTOR ALERT

The only thing harder than being a CEO in the global economy is being an investor. Every time I look at the growth in China, I'm tempted to drop everything and focus my investments there. Then I remember I know next to nothing about China. That's a problem.

Industries—and countries—that are growing rapidly are exciting. They invite bullishness. They also attract bad forecasts. When investing in any rapidly growing sector, it helps to understand that most forecasts are little more than a guess. Be skeptical. Use common sense.

When I first started my career, one of my bosses tried to teach us about common sense by describing a pitfall of demographic research: "Imagine if everyone in China bought just one bottle of Coca-Cola a month." You might think to yourself that one bottle of Coke a month per person is not a big assumption, but that the extra billion bottles a month would really help Coca-Cola's stock. Unfortunately, getting people to go from zero to one bottle a month is a giant leap, and generally takes a very long time. Common sense might have told you that people in China were not going to adopt fizzy drinks overnight, and you would have been right. In China, they prefer tea to fizzy drinks. Coca-Cola has done well in China, but China hasn't made a huge difference to the value of the stock.

The astonishing rates of growth in some emerging economies are so tempting. But remember the reality. Even the most exciting emerging economies are small, both in absolute terms and relative to their population. Per capita income in China in 2002 was only $960. But that number represents huge growth from only a few years earlier, and there seems to be little doubt that China will gradually—or not so gradually—work its way into the first tier of economic powers. The same may prove to be true for India and other emerging countries. Success in these emerging markets isn't going to happen overnight for anyone. In fact, for many American companies it won't happen at all. But that doesn't mean you can afford to ignore emerging markets. They are where the action is on both the supply and demand sides of the New Normal economic equation.

MAKING TECHNOLOGY WORK FOR YOUR COMPANY

No issue on the CEO's docket requires as much personal reprogramming as technology. We live in a technology-enabled time. If you are a CEO, you probably have staff people whose job it is to keep you up to speed. How many independent sources of insight do you have? You need to know how technology affects your business, and the fewer sources of insight you have, the more likely you are to miss something important. In order to be comfortable making strategic decisions driven by technology, you have to be conversant. Having a technology-savvy staff is important, but it is no substitute for understanding the issues yourself. If you delegate technology strategy, you may be disappointed by the outcome. And your shareholders may also be disappointed. If so, they may take out their disappointment on you. I know, you've heard this before and are probably confident that you're as up on technology as you need to be. Think about it again: Are you really?

Consider the example of the entertainment industry, where the Walt Disney Company has long been a leader. Beginning in the late 1980s, computer technology radically altered the cost of producing animated feature films, unleashing a new golden age of cartoons. After some early successes, Disney allowed itself to lose ground to upstarts such as Pixar and Dreamworks. Irony of ironies, both Pixar and Dreamworks excelled at integrating technology with storytelling to produce movies that out-Disneyed Disney and achieved blowout levels of success.

Elsewhere in entertainment, the recorded music industry also missed a huge opportunity. Having experienced fifteen years of unprecedented growth and profitability thanks to the compact disc, the record labels got complacent. They failed to understand the implications of the technology underlying the success of CDs. First came CD burners, then person-to-person sharing of digital music files. The record labels had no answer. Remarkably, they tried to pretend that nothing had changed. Ignoring the availability of a free alternative, they kept raising CD prices and resisted several efforts to create a legitimate alternative to piracy of digital files. The industry has come to see the error of its ways, but precious time and revenues have been lost.

How do you avoid a fate similar to these titans of entertainment? First, appreciate that technology is essential to business competitiveness. While technology is a bigger issue in some industries than in others, it is a factor everywhere. Technology is what makes globalization possible. It is the key to corporate productivity. It is central to product development and innovation. One of the oldest industries in the world is fishing, and few industries have seen a greater impact from technology. If you ever go sport fishing at a warm weather resort, check out the electronics on the boats. The fish have nowhere to hide.

If technology is not a core competence for your company today, the time has come to change that. The same goes for you, as CEO. You cannot afford to be ignorant of technology and its implications. To be clear, I am not suggesting that technology is the answer to all business questions. It's not. But technology is the newest and best tool available for achieving corporate goals. If you are less comfortable than you would like with technology—including the emerging technologies—this is a great time to get comfortable. The barriers to learning about technology are lower than ever, and the benefits to you are far greater. Where do you begin? You already know your business, and thanks to the Internet, you have access to almost everything that is known about technology. And you can do it from the privacy of your home or office.

If you're in a hurry, there are battalions of consultants eager to bring you up to speed. But that is just the first step. You also need to make sure those around you appreciate how important technology is. Every discussion of your business processes should include the following question: What technology is coming that will enable us to do this better, faster, or cheaper? A simple way to get your team on board with technology is for you to start wearing one of the new personal technologies, such as a BlackBerry for wireless e-mail, a cell phone with built-in camera, or an iPod for digital music. Your conspicuous use of such products will serve as a wake-up call for your team, telling them it's time to get with the program.

Second, technology works to the advantage of those who are closest to it. And it moves forward only because companies and individuals push it. If you want technology to help your company, you need to step forward and take charge of your company's technology future. Again, some industries are better positioned for this than others, but that is generally because they have taken technology seriously in the past.

Third, don't look for silver bullets. Technology is a tool, not an answer. You have to be very careful how you apply it. Vendors will make impressive promises, and your job is to get past the smoke and mirrors to the essence of what technology can do for your company. You need to have a strategic view of how technology fits into your business. You need to understand where technology can improve your business processes. This is not something that fits into a quarterly reporting cycle. It requires a planning horizon of three to five years. And it requires vision. If your vision is provided by a vendor, you may not be around to clean up the mess.

Fourth, when it comes to technology, the mainstream stuff can help you on the cost side, but leading-edge technology is the key to competitive advantage. If you're not sure whether a technology is leading edge, try the following test. If the vendor has revenues in excess of $1 billion and/or promises that the technology can be deployed today on an enterprise-wide basis, it's probably not leading edge. By definition, leading-edge products are not fully baked, so experimentation is essential to success. One of the key goals of the experiment is to ensure collaboration between your operating and information technology people. If your company is anything like the ones I know, such cooperation will not come naturally.

This leads to my fifth point, namely, that technology strategy cannot be imposed from the executive suite. Nor can it originate with your information technology (IT) organization. Every level of your organization should be involved to ensure that you combine an understanding of key business issues with insight about what is possible and cost-effective. Remember that the strategic view you have today is likely to be obsolete faster than you would like. They don't call this stuff technology for nothing. It changes all the time. The good news, though, is that it changes in ways that are relatively predictable. In that respect, technology is completely consistent with the New Normal. Flexibility really matters.

Remind your Chief Information Officer (CIO) that technology is key to your company's ability to survive and compete. No matter how smart it was to cut costs in information technology in the early years of this decade, it doesn't make sense to keep doing so. If you are going to increase shareholder value long term, your company must deploy technologies that contribute to that effort. This dictates a major change in the role of IT. As technology continues to move from the back office to the front, IT must collaborate with operating groups to ensure maximum effectiveness. Many IT people will claim they are already doing this, but I would ask them the following question: What role do operating groups play in determining which business processes get automated? Then ask the operating people the same question about IT.

Turf battles between IT and operating people have a long history, and they won't go away without special effort on your part. The key is to make sure that IT understands the strategic issues in your business and that operating people understand the issues associated with information technology. It won't happen overnight, but the investment you make today will pay dividends for the rest of your career.

The New Normal will reward companies that rethink their approach to IT. Viewing IT as an integrated part of your corporate strategy is the first step. Integrating IT into your business processes is the next. It's not enough to give your head of IT a C-level title. He or she has to *behave* like a C-level executive. Central to this approach is recognizing that market leaders have different opportunities than their competitors, but technology can level the playing field.

A case in point is the retail industry, where whining about Wal-Mart's scale advantages has become a favorite pastime. Even when Wal-Mart was a relatively small player, the company understood the importance of technology. It was an early adopter, spent more time studying its business processes than its competitors, and found ways to leverage technology for competitive advantage. Now Wal-Mart is the biggest retailer on the planet. Scale has huge advantages, but Wal-Mart's size inevitably makes change a slow process. The company has done a brilliant job of minimizing this. It will be interesting to see if any of Wal-Mart's competitors can use the coming wave of Web services technology to gain an edge.

PRESSURE TO PERFORM

I interact with dozens of CEOs, and with few exceptions they express tremendous frustration with investors and regulators. I share their frustration. Investors and regulators talk a great game about the long term and governance, but their actual behavior fails to live up to the talk. Investor time horizons in the public market have been getting shorter for at least twenty years. The impact of short-term trading on stock prices is so great that CEOs can be forgiven for thinking that no one really cares about the long term. The same is true with corporate governance. Shareholders generally don't behave like owners. If they don't like what is going on, they don't vote out management. They sell the stock.

Sadly, the regulators are little better. Where were the SEC and FASB when Enron, WorldCom, Tyco, and others were playing their games? They were quick to offer self-righteous condemnations of the bad guys after the fact, but they did nothing until it was too late to help the investors and employees who were harmed. What was really needed was better enforcement by regulators. Instead, we got regulatory reforms that penalize huge numbers of honest companies—and their investors—with little hope of preventing future frauds.

Thanks to Sarbanes-Oxley, boards of directors will be increasingly filled with "professional board members," most with fancy résumés and little interest in or appreciation for the details of the company's business. Great executives now are reluctant to take seats on other boards in the face of increased risk of litigation, and, given the threat of litigation, it is no surprise that boards are preoccupied with process. More than ever, board meetings are a triumph of form over substance. As a CEO in the New Normal, you need all the help you can get. Sarbanes-Oxley has probably enhanced the opportunity to populate your board with yes-men who know nothing about your business, but the New Normal has reduced the incentive to do so. The trick is to find capable people who are willing to join your board. When in doubt, opt for a smaller board. It will take less of your time.

One of my favorite examples of perversity of reform is the current passion for separating the role of board chairman from that of

CEO. I can think of lots of advantages to such a separation, but it seems to me that few of them will be realized unless the separation comes with a change in the CEO. This is what Dell Computer did when founder Michael Dell promoted his number two, Kevin Rollins, to the CEO job. Merely taking the chairman *title* away from a powerful CEO is likely to result in only superficial changes to governance, with little or no benefit to shareholders.

When added to the challenges of the New Normal, the pressure from shareholders and regulators makes the CEO's job harder than ever. You cannot ignore shareholders, nor can you allow them to drive your strategy. You have to manage their expectations. The trick here is to recognize that investors are smarter than their collective behavior might suggest, and they are very predictable. Investors own stocks to make money. They prefer to make money right now, but if the future is bright enough, they will be more patient than they get credit for. The key to success for CEOs is to strike a balance between the short and long term.

As CEO, your job is to give investors an incentive to be patient. If your plan requires you to nuke near-term earnings, you had better have a compelling plan. Otherwise, look for a more balanced approach. Investors understand J-curves. They understand that you have to invest now to create value in the long term. They just want you to be reasonable about it. If you don't really have a vision, get one. Investors have heard too many stories that didn't work, so be prepared for initial skepticism. Don't expect investors to buy into your vision until you've begun to deliver on it. Like everything else in the New Normal, investor relations should be integrated into your corporate strategy.

There is no way to avoid pressure from Wall Street to optimize short-run performance. But there are better and worse ways of handling that pressure. The first step is to remember that shareholders are entitled to their own view of what is best for the company. Ignoring them may be the right thing to do for the company, but there are consequences. Consider the case of Steve Jobs. Steve and his team restored Apple to financial health. He doesn't need to be as conservative as he's being right now. Apple has $4.6 billion in cash, only a small fraction of which it will ever need to run its business. In strictly financial terms, the right thing for Apple to do is to buy a ton of stock back so that the company's earnings are more valuable to shareholders. The reason Jobs is not doing that? The answer says something about the pressures facing CEOs. The first time Jobs was CEO of Apple—back in the mid-eighties—the company got into financial trouble and he was thrown out. He wants a nice big buffer to keep the company out of financial difficulty. Retaining $4.6 billion in cash is not the optimal thing for shareholders and they know it. The stock pays a penalty as a result.

One last piece of advice for CEOs: Whatever you do, don't mislead your investors. We live in an environment when honesty is more highly valued than ever. It's also an environment where business can deteriorate really quickly. When it does, think long term. Preserve your credibility. Get the bad news behind you. Hit a reset button and position your company for a better future.

.17.

THE INVESTING PLAYING FIELD IS (FINALLY) LEVEL

If you read enough newspaper accounts and watch enough market-related TV, you probably get the impression that Wall Street is rigged as never before. The volume of reports about conflicts, self-dealing, and other chicanery is truly disturbing. It reflects bad behavior by market participants, but also a lack of vigilance by regulators.

The recent flurry of enforcement actions reflects an aggressive campaign by the attorney general of the state of New York, Eliot Spitzer, who is attempting to fill a void left by lax enforcement by the Securities & Exchange Commission and the industry's self-regulatory organizations. From where I sit, it appears that Spitzer is having an enormously positive impact on Wall Street. The legal proceedings continue, but behavior on Wall Street has already improved dramatically—thanks to Spitzer's enforcement and because the benefits of bad behavior do not justify the risk. To find the silver lining to the clouds over Wall Street, look no farther than mutual funds, whose operators have improved their fees and service offerings in the wake of scandals. The only innocent parties who are entitled to be concerned about the new regulatory environment are corporate executives, who are getting numerous mixed signals about compliance.

Now's the time to make those scandals work for you. In my view, the playing field on Wall Street today still isn't perfect, but it's more level than at any time in history. In addition to the enforcement boom, a spate of new regulations and technology advances has chipped away at the advantages previously enjoyed by institutions. Before the immediacy made possible through the Internet and the recent Internet-mania-inspired regulations, institutional investors had a distinct edge in everything from access to information to transaction costs. Even if you had a corporate annual report FedExed to your front doorstep, you couldn't hope to match the near-real-time information available to professional investors. And when it came to conducting trades, individuals were generally at the back of a long line. Some of those disadvantages have now been eliminated, and the playing field's as level as it's ever been. Doing your homework can really pay off.

POWER TO THE PEOPLE

The dramatic increase in direct investment by individuals in the 1990s has radically altered the balance of power. In the days when Wall Street was the province of professionals, politicians showed little interest. They allowed the industry to regulate itself. Organizations of investment professionals, such as the New York Stock Exchange and the National Association of Securities Dealers, were responsible for keeping their members honest. They did a pretty good job in the days when Wall Street was primarily institutional, but they did not keep pace as individual investors gained influence. In the later years of the Internet mania, self-regulation fell short. Things have changed since the market's collapse. Politicians can no longer ignore Wall Street. Some, like Spitzer, are building political reputations as defenders of the individual investor. This political environment will be with us for many years to come. Politicians and the investment industry's self-regulatory bodies will compete with each other to see who can best champion the rights of the individual investor.

It is an enormously sad fact that so many people on Wall Street behaved badly in the late 1990s. It is an equally sad fact that regulatory enforcement proved to be inadequate to the task of policing the bad behavior when it occurred. So why am I so confident about the new, level playing field on Wall Street? There are two principal drivers of my positive outlook. First, in the late 1990s the financial markets were undergoing massive changes that can properly be labeled "once in a lifetime." Second, the principal structural change of the 1990s—the mass participation of individuals as direct investors—has raised the political importance associated with securities regulation to levels not seen since the 1930s.

To appreciate how much better the environment is today for investors—individual and otherwise—it's important to have some context about how regulation works. At the heart of the capital markets are individuals making choices. Each person acts in his or her own self-interest. When money is involved, some people lose touch with the rules. Greed sometimes overcomes good judgment. This is where regulation has to enforce fairness and restraint. There are rules to prevent abusive behavior, but those rules are based on two important factors: historical experience and self-policing.

Given how hard it is to predict the future anywhere—much

less in the capital markets—regulations cannot possibly anticipate changes in the market. For example, there was no way the Securities & Exchange Commission could have predicted the scale of the initial public offering (IPO) market in 1999 and 2000—two years that accounted for half of all the IPO money raised by technology companies from 1980 to 2003. Just as important, the number of participants in the capital markets is so great that there is no way for regulators to watch every move that every participant makes. Instead, what they do is try to create an environment where market participants have an incentive to do the right thing. Enforcement takes place on an exceptional basis. Most of the time the system works very well. In the late 1990s it didn't.

While market cycles have a great deal in common, about once a generation something happens that goes way beyond the circumstances contemplated by regulation. Either the rules prove inadequate or, more commonly, self-policing and enforcement break down. The mania of the late 1990s exposed flaws in the regulatory fabric, but ironically the problems had more to do with poor enforcement—both by the SEC and market participants—than with the regulations themselves. The existing regulations prohibited mutual fund executives from making after-hours market-timing trades in their own funds. The settlements to date indicate that SEC enforcement was inadequate. This is but one of many areas in which the SEC failed to live up to its mandate. I'm not overlooking the complete absence of judgment on the part of the executives involved. When rich people break the rules over small change, they are dumb, greedy, or both. It happened surprisingly often in the mania years.

FINANCIAL STATEMENTS THAT CONFUSE

Similarly, the Financial Accounting Standards Board (FASB), which presides over the Generally Accepted Accounting Practices (GAAP) standards used for financial reporting, deserves some blame for Enron and some of the other major frauds of the 1990s. Over the past twenty years, FASB tinkered constantly with GAAP. Some argued that the accounting rules of that time were too simplistic because they treated every company the same. But there were benefits to this simplicity. You could compare the financial statements of two companies with confidence that they had been prepared according to the same rules. Beginning in the late 1980s, FASB issued new standards designed to address industry-specific issues, as well as ones related to the proliferation of derivatives and other complex financial instruments.

In its attempt to cater to the specific needs of major industries, FASB made a huge number of changes to GAAP. Companies such as Enron and WorldCom appear to have exploited those changes to hide fraudulent financial behavior. The first of these standards to affect technology stocks was FAS 86, which related to the treatment of research and development for software. At the time, the prevailing industry practice was to expense software development. As I recall, essentially every company wrote off the cost of software development as it was incurred. This had the effect of depressing earnings—it was a conservative approach that eliminated any subjective judgment about the useful life of the software being developed. The problem was that IBM did not conform to the industry practice; they capitalized software development.

Sticklers for consistency that they are, the accounting standards board decided that it would make the industry conform to IBM's practice. Their justification was reasonable—after all, the useful life of software is typically several years—but the implementation of FAS 86 allowed for significant variation from company to company. Conservative companies typically assumed the shortest possible life for the software, whereas aggressive ones did the opposite. Overnight, it was harder to compare the financial statements of software companies.

Over the ensuing decade, FASB released dozens of other standards, touching on everything from accounting for income taxes and pension funds to off-balance-sheet financing. I should emphasize that many of the outrageous financing gimmicks that Enron used to fool investors were consistent with FASB regulations. By the mid-1990s, financial statements had become nearly indecipherable. To make matters worse, the regulations also changed to put financial reports in "plain English," which turned out to be a euphemism for gobbledygook.

When markets are out of control, and people are making money hand over fist, investors—and regulators—generally don't ask as many questions as they should. That is why Enron, Worldcom, Adelphia, and the other frauds got to be so huge before they were exposed. Rising stock prices also explain why investors so meekly accepted FASB's changes to financial reporting in the first place.

SUPPORT FOR REFORMS

A great deal of attention has also been directed at the rules governing IPOs, which were designed in times when IPOs were an insignificant and unexciting segment of the capital markets. In the first seventeen years of my career, IPOs never accounted for a meaningful portion of my funds' returns. There weren't very many IPOs in most of those years. IPOs generally didn't go up much. And my funds could never get enough shares to make a difference. As late as 1997, many institutional investors ignored IPOs, opting to wait six months to see how well each company did and buy the stock then. The rules for IPO allocations were straightforward: investment banks were required to allocate the shares to their best customers. The issuer could allocate up to 5 percent to "friends and family." Given the size and nature of IPOs in those days, the allocations to friends and family were not material.

By mid-1998, though, the Internet mania was in full swing, and the IPO market was explosive. IPOs often went up more than 100 percent the first day and kept going up from there. Shares in IPOs appeared to be found money. Demand grew and grew, and first-day price spikes got ever more outrageous. The flaws in the IPO process were exposed for all to see. Friends and family stock appeared to be a form of bribery by investment bankers, notwithstanding the fact that the bulk of the allocations were made by each IPO company's management. IPO pricing—long an imprecise balancing act designed to ensure active trading and, ideally, a rising stock price—suddenly looked like a conspiracy between investment banks and their best customers.

After the stock market collapsed in 2000, there was a groundswell of support for new regulations for the market as a whole, and for IPOs in particular. Two major pieces of reform legislation have emerged. First was Regulation Fair Disclosure (Reg. FD), which requires that public companies provide exactly the same level of disclosure to all investors, both institutional and individual. Reg. FD has radically altered corporate communications to investors. Companies now make transcripts of conference calls and analyst meetings available in real time to individual investors. Company executives have all but eliminated informal disclosure to institutional investors at conferences and trade shows. Most executives are now reluctant to say anything beyond what is in official public releases.

INVESTOR ALERT

Perhaps you have noticed situations where companies have reported dramatic news—either good or bad—only to see their stock price move in the direction opposite of what you would expect. Why does that happen? There is a Wall Street adage in play here: "Buy on the rumor, sell on the news." Stock prices reflect investor expectations about future earnings power, and values tend to be a function of both hard evidence and rumors. As a result, news is often anticlimactic. When a company announces a huge write-off, investors may push the stock up, thinking all the bad news is out. Conversely, investors may greet apparent good news with a sense that the future will be worse. The key, though, is that the market prices stocks based on all the available news. The market sometimes misinterprets situations, but you should be very careful before thinking that the market is wrong or that it doesn't understand. When people tell you, "Don't fight the tape," what they're saying is the market reflects real transactions made by investors. Both buyers and sellers are putting money behind their views. One of the most dangerous mistakes you can make is to think you are smarter than the market. If you don't have a significant advantage in terms of insights about a particular stock, you probably don't know more than the market.

The second piece of reform legislation was Sarbanes-Oxley, which primarily addressed corporate governance. I strongly support the objectives of Sarbanes-Oxley and hope the law works. But it raises a few concerns.

First, the law sets a standard for the largest companies and then holds companies of all sizes to that standard. This imposes a great financial and administrative burden on smaller companies. Only time will tell if the regulatory benefits justify the extremely high costs for smaller companies. Second, consider the cost to investors of implementing Sarbanes-Oxley. The example that follows is oversimplified but illuminating. There are six thousand publicly traded stocks, each of which will have to spend approximately $2.5 million to comply. At a market price-to-earnings ratio of 25, the cost of Sarbanes-Oxley—in terms of lost market capitalization—may be as much as $300 billion. For that price, the benefits had better be huge.

And then there are the intangible costs. Thanks to Sarbanes-Oxley, companies are forced to add people to their board who have less financial interest in the outcome of their decisions and less understanding of the details. I'm not saying boards were good before, but I am saying that Sarbanes-Oxley is unlikely to make them better. Finally, Sarbanes-Oxley creates the illusion that corporate governance problems can be resolved by separating the chief executive officer and chairman of the board. Separation might be good governance policy, but the idea that somehow it's going to make companies run better is ridiculous. To repeat a point I made in the chapter on CEOs, a lousy CEO who loses the chairman title will still be a lousy CEO.

BACK IN THE ENFORCEMENT BUSINESS

As I noted earlier, the regulations in existence prior to the mania actually addressed most of the wrongdoing that took place. So the big question now is just whether market participants can be trusted going forward. In the current enforcement environment, where Eliot Spitzer's team manages to be in several places at once, market participants have a much greater incentive to behave than they did a few years ago. Given the size and complexity of today's financial markets, though, we need more than the attorney general of the state of New York. The Securities & Exchange Commission has to get itself back in the enforcement business.

The political pressure on the SEC is intense. Spitzer has become something of a folk hero by standing up for individual investors. The SEC—the agency actually charged with protecting investors—must step up, too. This represents a major change in focus. In past market cycles, individual investors were only a small factor in the market. Not so today. Over the last decades, individual investor participation has grown from 30.2 million U.S. shareholders in 1980 to 84.3 million in 2002. Most of the 1980 participation was through mutual funds and the like. Individuals are now a meaningful part of overall market activity, and Congress will be particularly attentive to any perceived mistreatment. As a result, the SEC is on notice. Some at the SEC complain about budget constraints, but that's just politics. The SEC's enforcement budget is a significant multiple of Spitzer's. In the current climate, though, the SEC is likely to get more money, which will eliminate the excuse, if not the problem.

A better regulatory environment can definitely help individual investors, but that is only one element of the newly level playing field.

As in so many other sectors, consumers of financial services are reaping the benefits of both technology and service innovations. On the technology front, the Web has been transformational. I've already described the power of the Web as a tool for investment research. There is literally no limit to the primary research that anyone—individual investor or professional—can do on the Web. Essentially all companies have complete marketing materials available on the Web. This access enables you to learn about their products and services. Most also have recruiting pages that can provide you with a sense of the most promising sectors of the business. Other sites offer product analysis, comparative pricing, and other useful information. And thanks to Reg. FD, corporate Web sites have increasingly strong investor-relations sections. You can find everything from conference call scripts to presentations made at investor conferences.

In a matter of a few short years, individual investors have gone from being information disadvantaged to being buried in data. The trick now is to process it all. This is the problem institutional investors have faced all along. That's what I mean by a level playing field.

THE RESEARCH CONUNDRUM

Another area of regulatory reform relates to the way Wall Street firms manage research. Until thirty years ago, Wall Street commissions were regulated at exceptionally high levels, notionally to underwrite the cost of investment research. As with so many industries, deregulation came to Wall Street. Between 1975 and 2000, commission rates fell steadily, undercutting the profitability of trading and removing the subsidy for research. Recognizing a big opportunity to stimulate their merger and new-issue businesses, investment bankers stepped into the void and underwrote research. The product of this effort took two forms: large industrywide analyses that made no recommendations, and smaller company-specific reports that included forecasts and recommendations. The linkage between investment bankers and research analysts created the potential for conflicts, but institutional investors accepted those conflicts as the cost of getting good research.

The connection between investment bankers and research departments was actually a good thing. Any time I wanted to learn about a new industry or market segment, I could count on the availability of a thoughtful industry report from one firm or another. Some of these reports were a hundred pages or more. A couple—early Internet reports published by Morgan Stanley's Mary Meeker—were even published as trade paperbacks and sold in bookstores. Now that bankers no longer subsidize research, industry reports are fewer in number and lower in quality. At the company level, the story is pretty much the same. There is much less research coverage than there was a few years ago, and quality has deteriorated significantly.

In the years prior to Regulation FD, there was a widely held perception that the analyst at a company's primary investment bank had an information advantage. It was also understood that the analysts had insights that were not necessarily included in the research reports. So the ability to speak to the analysts was particularly valuable—and was something that was only available to institutions. One of the reasons that Reg. FD is good for individual investors is that it eliminates a lot of the information advantage sell-side analysts had. But what it hasn't done is eliminate the advantage institutions have in being able to talk to those analysts. They can still talk to them, but the analysts know less because companies aren't sharing as much information.

The other people who had advantaged access to research analysts were the traders at the analyst's firm. As commission prices fell, brokers looked for other sources of profit. One was "proprietary trading," which was trading for profit with the firm's capital. Think of it as a hedge fund within the brokerage firm. For a time, research analysts were compensated in part based on the profitability of their firm's trading desk. Recently, even that compensation link has begun to go away.

The recent regulation of Wall Street research has focused on the integrity of stock recommendations. While I admire the sentiment, I believe this focus is misplaced. Expecting Wall Street analysts to pick stocks is equivalent to asking sports writers to play in the games they are writing about. If analysts were great stock pickers, they would be running funds, not analyzing companies. Keep in mind that the biases in Wall Street research were very consistent, and it was straightforward for investors to filter them out. Recommendations were not meant to be taken literally—they were statements of relative enthusiasm. The problem came when a new and less experienced group of investors—individuals—gained access to the research. They forgot the adage "Let the buyer beware."

Due to the new regulations, investors no longer get a free ride on research. The standard Wall Street research that is available today is less plentiful and less substantial than what prevailed a few years ago. This is a much bigger problem for institutions than it is for individuals, who can't miss what they never had. Institutional investors are responding by relying more on internal research departments and commissioning proprietary research. A small industry has emerged to produce customized proprietary investment research for hedge funds and mutual funds. That's not an option available to most individual investors. Not yet, anyway. If you are concerned that institutions still have too great an information advantage over you, you can level the playing field by buying into a fund.

EVENLY DISTRIBUTED RECOMMENDATIONS?

One of the other perverse outcomes of reform relates to the distribution of investment recommendations. Regulators decided that analyst recommendations have to be distributed more or less evenly among buy, sell, and hold. The trouble is, that's not how the market works. In a bull market, most things go up. Forcing analysts to have an arbitrary percentage of sell recommendations puts us back where we were before: recommendations are just statements of relative enthusiasm. So please don't take analyst recommendations literally.

INVESTOR ALERT

Have you ever noticed how often Wall Street analysts raise their rating on a stock after it has already hit a new high? It seems as though it happens all the time. My advice is that you not pay attention to the rating itself, but rather to how the rating on a stock compares to other stocks that the analyst covers. Is it his or her favorite stock? Keep in mind, though, that being an analyst's favorite stock is no guarantee of future investment returns. These guys aren't portfolio managers, they're analysts.

Also, when you read Wall Street research, focus on the data, not the recommendation. Analysts are most useful for their ability to gather, interpret, and present information from diverse sources. Wall Street research is a great way to get up to speed on a new stock idea, but it is generally not enough. It's your job to decide which stocks are best suited to your portfolio, and to determine the optimal timing for purchase and sale.

Thanks to the new regulations, the playing field in research is level for all kinds of investors, but they all have to work harder. The institutions are working harder by hiring more analysts and paying third parties for custom research. Individual investors generally don't have the budget for custom research, so their best options are to leverage the institutions that do—by investing in mutual funds—or to devote more time and effort.

As a result of the reduction in research, the equity markets are less efficient than in the recent past. All else being equal, this increases the volatility of stock prices, which could actually be a plus for individual investors. If you do your homework, there is a greater probability that you'll discover something of value before it is well known to the entire world.

The Web has also provided great tools for trading. In reality, online brokerage has given individual investors a wide range of choices and capabilities. Brokers such as Charles Schwab and TD Waterhouse offer full-service solutions, with a focus on asset management, while Ameritrade and Scottrade focus on active traders. Whatever your needs, there is a broker—online or otherwise—ready to serve you. Because of the varying strengths of brokers, many individual investors have learned the benefits of multiple brokerage accounts, with each one targeting a specific application. This is no different than having one mutual fund for value stocks, another for emerging growth, and a third for international.

OVERCOMING TRANSGRESSIONS

Speaking of mutual funds, the renewed regulatory scrutiny is bound to have a significant impact on that industry. The recent scandals have cast a deep shadow that fund-management companies will struggle to remove for years to come. They will work doubly hard to earn back the trust of investors. While they are doing so, they may actually serve investors better.

It is quite possible that investors may benefit from the budding competition among fund-management companies for the status of most reformed. Several mutual fund companies took a step in this direction by announcing they would no longer would pay "soft-dollar" commissions to brokerages for research and other services. Soft dollars became popular following the deregulation of brokerage commissions in 1975. The idea behind soft-dollar payments is that a part of the commission paid by an investment manager to a brokerage is earmarked to pay for research and other services from a third-party vendor. The problem: like a lot of things in the investment business, a reasonable idea was taken too far. During the bull market, buy-side institutions used soft dollars to pay for everything from research to field trips to newspaper subscriptions to sports tickets. The effect was to use transaction commissions—commissions effectively paid by fund holders—to pay for goods and services that would otherwise have been cash expenses to the fund manager.

INVESTOR ALERT

The recent scandals regarding mutual funds caused great concern to many investors, some of whom are now avoiding mutual funds out of fear that there will be more scandals. I don't think this is the high-percentage response. It's quite possible that increased regulatory scrutiny will reveal more past transgressions, but I suspect that current behavior in the mutual fund business is very good. The fund business has historically enjoyed a well-deserved reputation for integrity. Many firms—including some of the industry's largest—have come through the recent scandals untouched. My view is that this is probably a great time to be a mutual fund investor. Some of the funds that were touched by the scandals have reduced their fees and improved their customer service. Every firm is more attentive to compliance, as well as performance and service.

While mutual funds dominate the investment landscape, a lot of power has shifted to hedge funds. Today there are literally thousands of hedge funds. While they're much smaller than mutual funds—most of them manage a few hundred million in assets or less—they trade with an intense velocity. Whereas a typical mutual fund might turn over its portfolio twice a year, a hedge fund might do it once or twice a month. The result: mutual funds are no longer pricing stocks. Hedge funds are. And hedge funds are trading in—and pricing—small cap and micro cap stocks. You might have assumed that because mutual funds are so huge and invest in companies whose market capitalization can handle them—the top three hundred or so companies—that it's wise to invest in smaller companies, which are free of influence from mutual funds. But keep two things in mind. First, that the hedge funds might be there, wielding more power than ever. Second, that smaller companies are, by nature, less stable than large companies. So you have to do more work and pay more attention to them. There are more ways they can disappoint you.

Sure, institutions still have the upper hand. But they have issues to deal with, like too much capital and too many distractions. On the other hand, you, as an individual investor, have a lot working in your favor. The Internet gives you access to far more information than you've ever had before. You can become better educated about the industries and companies where you might want to invest your money. Also, as a consumer, you're the ultimate customer for products sold by an increasing number of companies you might consider for investing. You're in a prime position to judge for yourself whether a company's product is a winner or loser. And you've got new tools at your disposal to give you more equality, like brokerage firms that focus on execution and charge really low pricing for individual transactions.

In most of the major areas of Wall Street—including disclosure, research, trading, corporate governance, mutual funds, and enforcement—the playing field is more level than ever, which is great for individual investors. Yes, there are still issues and inconsistencies in both securities regulations and in brokerage services. But in all cases the situation is more constructive than in the past. Investing still isn't easy—remember that you are competing with people who do this for a living—but at least it's fair. There has never been a better time to be an individual investor.

.18.

NEW RULES FOR WINNING ON WALL STREET'S LEVEL FIELD

I was not destined to be a technology investor. I majored in American history in college, where I took only two classes in engineering. In business school, I took a minicourse on computer programming . . . and didn't like it. I became a technology investor by accident—it's what T. Rowe Price needed when I arrived—and had to work like crazy to make myself successful. If it worked for me, it can work for anyone.

Today, it's easier than ever. The economy is changing dramatically, giving individual investors not only huge amounts of influence over the market but also advantages previously available only to professional investors—all the advantages I outlined in the previous chapter. Regulatory reform, in combination with an unprecedented array of investment tools and services, improves the chances of success for everyone.

We're going to need it. In the years ahead, we will all have to take on more responsibility for our wealth management. We no longer can count on the government to take care of us. I'm not suggesting that Social Security is going away. I don't believe that. Politics will protect Social Security—and Medicare—at some level, but probably not at the level we would like. We need to make up the difference. And guess what? We're living longer, so we will need more money for retirement.

There are lots of options for building a retirement nest egg—or financing a child's education or an aging parent's care. The important thing is to adopt an approach that fits into your life and achieves your financial objectives.

My goal with this chapter is to offer you a road map for successful investing. My expertise is in buying and selling stocks, so that's where I will focus most of my effort. But there is more to wealth management than picking stocks, so I will give you my best insights about the other key steps you should follow.

There are many ways to perform well as an investor, whether in the stock market or other markets. There are people who are successful with almost every strategy under the sun. What they have in common is two things: discipline and luck. By discipline, I mean that they implement their strategy in a methodical way over a period of years. And I'm not discounting the necessity of good fortune. There's a well-worn adage in the investment business on this subject: "If you have the choice of being smart or lucky, always choose lucky."

The investment methodology I favor emphasizes fundamental research, patience, and common sense. This approach does not provide the thrills that come with momentum investing, but the returns have been excellent. My funds employ what amounts to a "buy-and-hold" strategy. My objective in this chapter is not to convince you of the merits of my approach but rather to use my methodology as a framework to help you decide on the best approach for you.

Over the years, I have evolved fifteen rules that govern my investment behavior. These rules are the collected scar tissue from twenty-two years of technology investing. They worked for me at T. Rowe Price Associates. They have worked for me at Integral and Silver Lake. I use them at Elevation. I always make adjustments to fit the situation, but the rules live on. To be clear, these rules have not prevented me from making mistakes and losing money. But consistently applied, in combination with hard work, they have contributed to my success.

During my years in the mutual fund business at T. Rowe Price, I had to deal with a stock market that didn't like technology. These were the early days of personal computers, and for every dollar investors made in Microsoft and Compaq, they seemed to be losing two dollars in IBM, Digital Equipment, and other old-line companies. From this environment, the rules emerged.

In 1990 I realized that the innovation in Silicon Valley—and Microsoft Windows—would eventually produce a bull market in technology stocks. That's when John Powell and I joined forces with Kleiner Perkins Caufield & Byers to start Integral Capital Partners. The nineties were a great period for technology investing, and the rules helped me make the most of them.

By 1997 I became concerned about manic behavior among technology investors. Almost three years before the market's peak, things were already out of control. I couldn't imagine a soft landing and was convinced that my fund would not be able to escape a market collapse. We needed to diversify our business. That's when Jim Davidson, David Roux, Glenn Hutchins, and I concocted Silver Lake, a new type of fund that would be successful in whatever environment followed the Internet mania, the environment that turned out to be the New Normal.

The strategy at Silver Lake was to make large-scale investments in established market leaders in technology and related growth industries. The idea was to invest in really good companies that were out of favor with investors, then help management improve the business. With an investment-time horizon of five to seven years, Silver Lake could take advantage of Wall Street's tendency to value companies based largely on near-term results.

Silver Lake is optimized for the New Normal. The fund spends months or even years on research and due diligence prior to making investments. It only invests in companies that have both a solid core business and opportunities to grow. Silver Lake is extremely careful about the price it pays when it invests. After the investment, Silver Lake behaves like a partner to management—rather than a trader. The Silver Lake team helps each portfolio company improve its business and take advantage of growth opportunities.

Recently I collaborated with Fred Anderson, Marc Bodnick, Bono, Bret Pearlman, and John Riccitiello to launch Elevation Partners. Like Silver Lake, Elevation invests in established market leaders, but it focuses on the media and entertainment industry. Technology has transformed media and entertainment—particularly on the content side of the business—creating what we believe are attractive investment opportunities. We are very long term in our approach. We partner with management to improve business processes and leverage technology for competitive advantage.

While you can't invest in Silver Lake or Elevation, you can learn from the approach we have taken, an approach to investing that is tailored to the New Normal environment. Here are my rules. Some will be obvious to you. Others may be new. Some will work for you, others may not. But these are the rules that I use every day. They are the rules I use to train new members of my team.

Rule #1: Know Yourself

While investment programs are not as unique as fingerprints, they should be highly customized. Start by defining the goals of your investment program and determining your time horizon. If your investment program needs to fund your children's education or care for aging parents, the approach is likely to be different than if it is just for your retirement—you may not have as much wiggle room. The next thing to figure out is your risk profile. Are you the kind of person who can't sleep at night when an investment declines in value? If you are, don't be embarrassed. Just limit the volatility of your investments. The nature of markets is such that you can lose money so much faster than you can make it. If you are going to make a mistake with respect to risk profile, be too conservative. It's generally easier to recover from that mistake.

One of the most important things to know about yourself is how interested you are in the investment process itself. How much time are you prepared to devote to your investment activities? Does investing excite you enough to justify a meaningful portion of your free time? If not, there are many able professionals who can help you achieve your investment objectives. There are also many books, magazines, and Web sites that can help you identify the package of services and professionals that is right for you.

The great investor Peter Lynch expressed dismay that most people put less thought into picking stocks than they do into acquiring a major appliance. My own experience confirms this, and not just among individual investors. Believe it or not, investment professionals, too, have been known to fall victim to such lax behavior.

Like just about everything else in the New Normal, the world of investments presents a daunting array of choices. I prefer to keep things simple, and I recommend that you do the same, at least as you begin. Think of investment choices as a continuum of risk, with Treasury bills being the least risky investment and derivatives (such as options and futures) as the most risky. Bonds and stocks are in between, but spread across the spectrum. If you know what you are doing, you will earn a rate of return from each class of securities that compensates you for risk. The trick is to know what you are doing. You are competing with people who do this for a living, people with enormous resources at their disposal. Before you buy cocoa futures, realize that the counterparty to your trade may be Hershey or M&M/Mars.

There are professional investors in every category of Wall Street, but not all of them have the advantages that Hershey has in chocolate or ExxonMobil in oil. Regulatory reform has eliminated many of the advantages held by Wall Street professionals, particularly in equities. Individual investors also benefit from the fact that America's fastest-growing industries are increasingly orienting themselves toward consumers. In my experience, it's a whole lot easier to understand investment opportunities for companies of which you are already a customer.

Rule #2: Determine an Allocation of Assets

Your age, risk tolerance, and investment objectives will influence the appropriate mix of assets in your portfolio—your combination of real estate, stocks, bonds, and mutual funds.

When people learn that I am a technology investor, they assume that I favor high-risk investing. That's not actually the case. Remember that I became a tech investor only because my first employer needed a technology analyst. Over the years, I learned everything I could about the technology industry and industries affected by technology, and media including media and entertainment. After a while, technology and media became second nature to me. I invest in tech and media businesses because they are what I know best. My knowledge and experience reduce the risk. In fact, for me, technology and media stocks are relatively low-risk investments.

Rather than investing in sectors I don't know, I simply split my investments between T-bills and technology and media, adjusting the relative weight according to my risk tolerance.

The rest of my rules address the portion of your portfolio that is devoted to direct ownership of stocks.

Rule #3: Focus Pays

There are thousands of public companies in the United States alone. There is no way to keep track of more than a few dozen, and only then if you are prepared to devote a lot of time to research. So the question is, How do you decide where to focus your energy?

Like most of my rules, I learned about this one the hard way. When I first began in 1982, I was assigned to two groups within technology: software and defense electronics. As a brand-new analyst, I had no clue what I was doing and had no idea how to allocate my time between the two groups. I struggled for a few months until my boss made it clear I was not doing a good job. He didn't tell me what to do, but I knew that I had to do something dramatic or I'd be out of work. Even before that conversation, I knew I was struggling. What I needed was advice, and permission to follow it. That's what I got. The next day, I dropped one of my two groups, focused all of my energy, and learned how to be an analyst.

Rule #4: Some Businesses Are Inherently Better Positioned Than Others, and the Same Is True for Stocks

When I talk to other investors, I am constantly surprised at how many focus on near-term business momentum to the exclusion of everything else. Too many people seem to think that momentum is the only thing that matters.

Momentum is a good thing, but momentum investing is extremely time consuming. Momentum requires positive news flow, and staying ahead of positive news flow is a full-time job best done by relatively large organizations with lots of capital. I am not suggesting that momentum investing won't work for individuals but rather that it is far riskier for individuals than for institutions whose buying power can contribute directly to sustaining momentum. If you really believe in momentum as a strategy, I believe your best move would be to buy into mutual funds or hedge funds that have a demonstrated record of success with it.

For individuals whose time is limited, other strategies of direct investing may be more appropriate. One example would be value investing, where you buy out-of-favor securities that are priced below their intrinsic worth. If you prefer growth-stock investing, I would propose two rules of thumb. First, good timing has a huge impact on returns. When a growth stock has a demonstrated track record, investors will generally pay a premium. When that is the case, you may be better off waiting for a market decline or a company-specific disappointment before buying shares. The second rule of thumb is to know what you are buying. For the kind of growth stock investing that I practice, the most important factor is the ability to tell the difference between great, good, and mediocre companies. You can make money in any stock if your timing is right. The better the company, though, the less precise your timing needs to be.

So what is the secret to good positioning?

When I want to figure out which companies are best positioned, I start by asking a single question: Whose products are most indispensable? In the PC market, for example, Microsoft's operating systems and Intel's microprocessors are found in more than 90 percent of all machines. On the Internet, the short list of indispensable products today includes communications devices (made by Cisco and others), browser software (made by Microsoft), search engines (made by Google), and marketplaces (from eBay and others).

To assess whether customers will pay a premium, compare a company's income statement to those of its competitors and to the best companies in other sectors. The margins at Microsoft, Intel, Cisco, Google, and eBay are much higher than their competitors. They are also higher than companies of comparable size in other industries. Being well positioned is not the same thing as being a good stock, but it's a start.

Assessing management is tricky. On the one hand, financial statements provide significant clues about management quality. If a company delivers superior financial results over a long period of time, you can probably conclude that management has played a role. Keep in mind, though, that growth is not enough. It's also critically important that the balance sheet be sound. Unfortunately, financial statements tell only part of the story. It is far trickier to predict future success in a rapidly changing economy. As a result, I continually assess management's performance in terms of financial results, product innovation and quality, and other factors.

Just because one company has better metrics than another does not mean that its stock will necessarily do better. Some companies are known to be excellent and are priced accordingly. Microsoft and eBay are examples. You can make money on such stocks, but you have to be careful about when you buy them, and you have to hold them for a long time. Ironically, some lesser companies can provide superior investment returns simply because investor expectations are lower. When they surprise on the upside, investors are *truly* surprised, which causes prices to rise. From time to time, a company can transition from the second tier to the first. A great example is Dell, which until the early 1990s was a scrappy player—with poor financial controls—in the rapidly growing PC sector.

Once Dell upgraded its financial management and perfected the direct model of selling PCs, though, the company was unstoppable. Wall Street eventually recognized the change and accorded the company a much higher price-earnings multiple. Investors who held Dell stock during this transition did fabulously well.

Rule #5: Some Business Models Are Inherently Superior

The best companies have three things going for them. They are well positioned for the future. They sell products or services for which customers will pay a premium. And they have management that is ideally suited to the situation. Premium products in the hands of a great management team translate into a superior business model.

Companies with high margins, high market share, significant intellectual property protection, and low capital intensity are far more likely to be successful than those without. For example, a disk drive vendor serves the same market as Microsoft, but its business model pales by comparison. My funds have made lots of money in disk drive stocks, but it has taken far more work than with Microsoft.

All else being equal, I prefer companies that sell millions of units of a low-priced product through indirect channels over ones that sell a low-volume, high-priced product through a direct sales force. Microsoft would be an example of the former; Oracle of the latter. Both models can produce good businesses—Microsoft and Oracle are examples—but direct-sales models are more subject to negative earnings surprises.

The better the business model, the more resilient a company is in tough times. Microsoft's business is no longer growing very fast, but the company continues to generate prodigious profits and cash flow. As a consequence, it maintains a high valuation. Dell, which operates in the same industry as Microsoft, has a less attractive business model, but superior growth dynamics. The reason is that Dell is gaining share relative to Hewlett-Packard, IBM, and the other major vendors of PCs. And relative to those vendors, Dell has a superior business model.

Dell sells directly to customers—bypassing distributors and retailers—with three huge benefits. First, Dell does not have to invest in inventory to be held by distributors and retailers. This makes Dell far more capital-efficient than its competitors. Second, because it has no channel inventory, Dell can bring new products to market and get them into the hands of customers much faster than competitors. In an industry where new features really matter, that is a big deal. And lastly, Dell receives its payment directly from customers—rather than in steps through a distribution channel—which means it requires essentially no capital to fund growth. Dell has executed its business model brilliantly. No wonder that company has gained so much market share.

The experience of Dell in the 1990s illustrates a key aspect of stock valuation. Price/earnings (P/E) multiples are highly correlated with both the level of and changes in profit margins. When a company's margins are very high, the multiple tends to be high, but it rarely expands unless margins are rising. Conversely, low-margin businesses tend to have low P/E multiples. For all companies, the multiple tends to rise as margins rise, and fall as margins fall. There are no absolutes, though. The stock market has fashions—just like any other sector—and there are times when it values businesses in ways that cannot be explained with numbers.

You can make a lot of money in stocks where the business model is nothing special, but your timing has to be excellent. The key is to identify situations where margins are expanding and growth is accelerating.

Rule #6: Insight Is Precious

In the stock market, information is a commodity. There is so much information out there that what you really need is a filter to help you focus on the important stuff. Insight is the filter that keeps us from drowning in data. It is also the filter that enables us to make money. When I lose money on a stock, I always try to understand what I got wrong. Almost every time, I discover that I had the key pieces of information but had not given them the proper weight in my analysis. I call that a failure of insight.

I have been blessed to have several important insights in my career. The really big ones led to the formation of Integral in 1991 and Silver Lake in 1999, as well as the liquidation of Integral III right at the top of the market in 2000. Other insights were about individual stocks. These were not life-changing choices, but without them I would have been far less successful.

In 2000 the market began its postmania collapse. Silver Lake was considering an investment in Datek Online, a major player in the online brokerage business. It seemed risky to buy into a brokerage business at the beginning of a bear market. The conventional wisdom also suggested that online brokers were creatures of the bull market and would not survive a downturn. These factors made us very cautious.

Our research provided two important insights that changed our view and ultimately caused us to invest in Datek. First, twenty years earlier, discount brokers—the online-equivalent brokers of that era—had gained share throughout their first bear market, suggesting that online brokers might leverage their superior value proposition to produce a similar outcome. Second, our due diligence indicated that Datek's technology was not just the best among online brokers, but was also a compelling Internet application by any standard. Armed with these insights, we realized that Datek's superior technology might enable the company to gain market share and prosper during a bear market, which is precisely what happened. Datek was profitable every month of the bear market, and it may have been the only brokerage in the country that can say that. In 2002 the company merged with Ameritrade to create the largest online brokerage firm in the world. And despite a monster bear market, the company prospered, and we had a very successful investment.

In 1993 my partners at the venture-capital firm of Kleiner Perkins Caufield & Byers held an offsite to discuss investment opportunities related to what was then known as Digital Convergence. There was a widely held belief in those pre-Internet days that the technology of computers, television, and telecommunications was coming together. As the leading venture firm in Silicon Valley, Kleiner Perkins had tremendous insights about Digital Convergence, and I attended their periodic offsites to test existing insights and gather new ones.

The insight I needed to test was that Digital Convergence would trigger huge demand for database software. Kleiner Perkins agreeded with the insight, but they did not plan to invest in any database software companies. When I asked why not, they explained that they did not see an opportunity for new companies because Oracle's software would do the job very effectively. Oracle was still in the early stages of recovery from a financial train wreck, and its stock was very reasonably priced.

If Kleiner Perkins wasn't going to fund a company to compete with Oracle, then the only competition would come from existing players such as Sybase and Microsoft, competitors that Oracle seemed well prepared to handle. That was a new and very valuable insight. As an owner of Oracle, I felt renewed confidence in the stock. Over time, I bought more of it. When the Internet revolution started a couple years later, Oracle was perfectly positioned.

You don't have access to Kleiner Perkins's offsites the way I did in 1993, but you do have access to something almost as important: Google. Google allows you to search the Internet for competitors and all manner of interesting insights, wherever they may reside. For example, you can search the Web sites of Kleiner Perkins, Sequoia Capital, and the other leading venture firms to see where they are putting their money . . . and just as important, where they are not. The former will give you a sense of where venture firms perceive public companies are unlikely to be successful. The latter demonstrates where venture investors see no opportunity, either because public companies are too entrenched or because the future holds no promise. Venture investors are not always right, but you can count on them to put their money behind their best ideas.

Keep your mind open. Insights don't wave a flag in front of your face.

Rule #7: It All Comes Down to Products

Wall Street puts a huge amount of effort into forecasting revenue and earnings, yet the track record of those forecasts is terrible. I believe that spreadsheet software—Microsoft Excel—is a major factor. When analysts make forecasts, they base them on a set of assumptions. The act of converting the assumptions into numbers on a spreadsheet—with automated calculations—is accompanied by a subtle tendency to eliminate spikes. How often do Wall Street revenue forecasts show consistent rates of growth? Very often. How often do companies actually grow at a consistent rate? Seldom. That's why I don't pay attention to Wall Street forecasts.

Whether the company you are looking at is small or large, new or old, understanding the products will make a big difference to your rate of return. My rule of thumb is this: If a product is hot, Wall Street's earnings estimates will always be too low. If the product isn't hot, the estimates will prove to be too high. Because of this, I spend most of my time analyzing the products themselves. I tend not to worry about price/earnings multiples until they expand beyond all historical precedent. The less diversified the company, the better this approach works.

When it comes to analyzing products, stick to those you understand. You may miss a few hot stocks, but in the long run you will make far more money.

Rule #8: For Growth Stocks, Product Cycles Are the Cycles That Matter

Economists talk about interest rates and the economic cycle, which are very important to the mature industries of our economy. But if you invest in growth stocks, product cycles are what matter most. Most products have a limited life, and most follow a relatively predictable life cycle.

The first phase of that cycle targets early adopters, people who are willing to pay a premium for access to the latest and coolest products. Success with early adopters enables a vendor to gain economies of scale in manufacturing, lower its price, and boost sales volume. The second phase, expansion, has a particularly attractive combination of growth, volume, and profitability. This is where the big money gets made, both by the company and by investors. The final, maturity phase requires significantly lower prices to appeal to late adopters, with consequently lower margins and growth.

To maximize my success as an investor, I try to identify hot products as early as possible in the life cycle. Identifying a hot product in the start-up phase is exceptionally rewarding but very hard to do. At this stage, the big risk is that the product won't live up to expectations. Falling short of expectations is never good for a stock. How bad it is depends on the size of the miss and the number of disappointed investors. Waiting until a product is in the expansion stage reduces risk, but it also lessens the potential upside. If you make an investment relatively early in the expansion phase, though, you are likely to be rewarded with excellent returns. In the maturity phase, the risk-reward is very unfavorable, with little upside and big potential downside.

Product-cycle investing works best with small and medium-sized companies, as well as with large companies with limited product lines. Intel is an example of the latter. Each generation of Intel microprocessor has a product cycle that accounts for huge swings in the stock price. Intel's ability to minimize the disruption of product transitions has materially enhanced its price/earnings multiple.

Don't fret if you can't identify hot products during the early adopter phase. For the truly great companies, you can miss a surprising amount of the early growth without missing the big returns. Consider the case of Microsoft. The company went public in 1986. Between 1986 and 1990, when Microsoft introduced Windows 3.0—the version that caused Windows to become a standard—the stock went from $21 to $71.50 after two two-for-one stock splits. If you bought the stock at the end of 1990, six months after Windows 3.0 shipped, your return over the next decade would have been 2,067 percent.

Product transitions cause uncertainty . . . and create buying windows even in the best-positioned companies. Strong product cycles also provide opportunities for trading profits in companies that are relatively poorly positioned. The key, though, is not to confuse a strong product cycle with good positioning or a product transition with the end of a company's opportunity.

Rule #9: Decimal Points Don't Matter

This rule has a corollary: Never play for pennies. The opportunities for well-positioned technology companies are so big—and last so long—that you should not set arbitrary buy or sell targets. Wall Street analysts almost always have price targets, but I pay no attention to them. With the exception of one five-month period in 1994, I have owned Cisco continuously since it went public in 1990. I have owned Oracle continuously since 1992. I have owned Dell since 1993. I would have been better off unloading all three in early 2000, but even with the price compression since 2000 I am better off than I would have been had I paid attention to price targets in any year from 1995 to 1998. At Silver Lake, every investment we make has a time horizon of at least five years. Think about that. We bought Seagate—a disk drive company—knowing that we probably would not be able to sell the bulk of our shares for five years or more. We did the same thing with Datek at the beginning of a bear market. The key in both cases was that our initial price compensated us for the risk of a long holding period.

When I buy a stock, I try to use dollar cost averaging, which is the practice of buying positions in increments over a period of weeks or months. I generally do not sell a stock until the company's position in its market begins to deteriorate. Only rarely do I sell a stock just for valuation reasons. The one exception was in the first quarter of 2000, when Integral liquidated its largest fund and distributed the cash to our investors. At that time, we were troubled by the manic behavior of Wall Street and decided it was best to reduce our assets under management.

Rule #10: In Making Investment Decisions, Do Not Rely on Management Guidance Alone

Many of my most costly investment mistakes came when I listened to management, rather than to my gut. I'll never forget the day in 1990 when Oracle announced that for the first time since it went public four years earlier, it would fail to grow at least 100 percent year over year. Oracle's balance sheet had been deteriorating for more than a year—a major red flag—as it struggled to sustain an impossibly high growth rate. The signals of trouble were everywhere, but I continued to rely on management's assurances that everything was fine. The stock had done so well that I didn't want to miss further upside if Oracle continued to make its numbers. For a while the strategy worked. When it stopped working, the price drop wiped out all of my prior gains and then some. *Ouch.* The only good thing I did was to hold on to part of the position until the company came back.

I find that management is often the last to know—and certainly the last to tell—when there is a problem in its business. From a research perspective, company executives are most useful as a check on competitors. The corollary to this for individual investors is, Do not rely on a broker's guidance alone. Use common sense. Do your own work. Try the products. Make your own decisions.

In this era of Regulation FD, institutional investors no longer have the advantage of access to management. Management teams are much more careful when they speak to investors, but that doesn't keep some CEOs from touting their stock. Be forewarned.

Rule #11: Balance Research Insights with Opportunism

Research determines what should be done, but the market determines what *can* be done today. What I mean by this is that the best-positioned technology stocks are often expensive, but they are still subject to volatility. The market is so focused on near-term results that minor disappointments often produce huge swings in value. This is precisely how I invest in technology stocks. I identify great companies and then wait for some shortfall before I buy. If you are willing to buy the best-positioned companies when others are selling, you will be rewarded.

Silver Lake's investment in Seagate Technology is an example of this. Seagate is the world's largest vendor of hard disc drives, but when we invested in 2000, the company's biggest asset was a one-third ownership of Veritas, the largest vendor of software for storage management. Seagate owned $20 billion worth of Veritas at a time when its own market capitalization was a mere $14 billion. The gap was roughly equal to the tax hit associated with selling the Veritas stock. In other words, Wall Street placed a value of zero on the world's largest disc drive business.

The deal we worked out resulted in Veritas buying Seagate at an all-time high and distributing Seagate's Veritas shares to shareholders on a tax-free basis. A Silver Lake–led investor team and Seagate's management team bought the disk drive business. The deal was possible because Veritas's stock price was so high and Veritas was concerned about the possibility that someone would buy Seagate to get control of Veritas. We seized the moment and offered a solution that was optimal for shareholders, for employees and management, for Veritas . . . and for us. Many of our investors thought we were crazy to buy a disk drive business. Our view was that Seagate was the best company in a tough business, that the Internet would make storage more important, and that new markets would give Seagate significant new growth opportunities. In one of the worst market environments in history, we made a very big return.

Rule #12: A Perfectly Diversified Technology Portfolio Is Bound to Underperform

Every few years a new technology industry comes along that captures investors' fancy. When it does, investors bid up the stock of every company in the industry. Over time, though, one of two things happens. If the new industry fails to materialize, all the companies disappear. If the industry thrives, customers ultimately narrow their purchases to a handful of vendors. In some industries, a single vendor winds up with a monopoly or near monopoly. When that happens, every other stock in the sector lags or falls away.

Technology industries are ruthlessly Darwinian, ultimately winnowing out all but a handful of companies. The challenge for investors is to diversify away the ever-present risk of execution problems—bad management, product transitions, and the like—without diversifying into less attractive businesses. If you think that Web services is going to outperform the tech industry and the stock market, for example, your list of beneficiaries might include enterprise players such BEA Systems, IBM, Microsoft, and Citrix Systems. There are other players, but these are the big ones. Unfortunately, IBM and Microsoft are so large that even a big win in Web services might not be meaningful. At this point it's hard to know which company will emerge the winner—it may be a new player altogether—but a portfolio that includes all of the early leaders is likely to include the one that ultimately wins. If your insight about Web services proves to be correct, even the secondary names in the sector will prove to be superior stocks to companies in other sectors, at least for a time. And as the winner makes itself known, you can reduce positions in the also-rans.

The most extreme example of this Darwinism is venture capital. The typical venture capital firm makes thirty to fifty investments per fund over the course of three years. They hope the best investment they make provides a return equal to the original value of the fund. They hope the next best five investments collectively provide a similar return. If the next best ten investments do the same, then the fund is a winner, even if the rest of the deals—fourteen to thirty companies—amount to nothing. It's a very high risk approach to investing, and it depends on the venture capitalist's ability to help portfolio companies achieve success.

Rule #13: Avoiding Losers Is as Important as Picking Winners

Even in the public market, there are far more losers than winners. They are costly. They are demoralizing.

In my experience, a surprising number of the stocks recommended to me by others fail to perform. Way too many of them go down. Some go down a lot. As a result, I do my own work before buying a stock. That's usually the best way to steer clear of losers. I wish I could say I had always avoided losers. I haven't. There were years—1990 and 2001 come to mind—when a small number of really big losers killed my performance.

When you are looking for potential losers, consider a few simple questions:

- How substantial is the business? Is it consistent from quarter to quarter?
- What is happening to profit margins?
- Has there been any balance sheet deterioration? If accounts receivable rise faster than sales, that's an indication of a deterioration. What is happening to cash?
- How promotional is management?

In my experience, there is no way to avoid losers. The best you can hope for is to identify them early and eliminate the positions before they cause you too much damage. This is a lot easier said than done. When a company reports disappointing results, investors typically react emotionally. In some cases, they overreact. Before acting, the central question you should try to answer is this: Was the bad news a one-time event or a signal of a larger problem? If the former, then the correct tactical response is to buy more shares, as the price decline creates a window of value. If the problem is likely to persist, however, you can count on more bad news and further price declines. In that case, sell as quickly as you can. Either way, though, keep emotion out of the decision-making process.

Rule #14: There Is Only One Microsoft

Don't waste your time looking for the next Microsoft. By the time the next Microsoft achieves that position, you will have missed years of stock appreciation. If you invest in the best-positioned companies in the most attractive industries, the "next Microsoft"—should one emerge—will already be in your portfolio when everyone finally recognizes the stock for what it is. This is the same lesson I conveyed in my example above about Web services.

These days, Wall Street is talking about Google. With more than a billion dollars in sales and operating margins of more than 30 percent prior to its initial public offering, Google is one of the best-performing businesses in the history of Silicon Valley. It went from start-up to a "verb" in five years. Google is as good a candidate for the title of "next Microsoft" as any, but ironically that may not be enough to make it a great stock. Google is so well known and expectations are so high that it may be hard for the company to live up to its promise. So not only do I want you to stop looking for the "next Microsoft," I want you to stop looking for the "next Google" also.

Rule #15: Don't Focus on the IPO Market

The IPO market in 1998 and 1999 was like a lottery in which every player won. Unfortunately, those were the only two years like that in my entire career. Even so, it seems as though everyone wants to believe the IPO market is where the action is on Wall Street. That is not my experience.

The major problem with the IPO market: it's tiny. There aren't very many good IPOs. What's worse, the good IPOs tend to be small, which means that few people get shares. And those who are allocated shares don't get enough to make a difference. It's hardly worth the effort.

The really big money in investing comes from buying the stocks of great companies and holding them for a period of years. Microsoft, eBay, and Intel were all IPOs once, but you could have bought them just about any time since and done extraordinarily well.

CONCLUSION

Now that you've had an opportunity to look inside the New Normal, I have a question to ask: Would you rather be living now or in another time?

I know my answer.

I can't imagine a time as exciting as this one. We live in an era full of possibilities. Technology and globalization have created new rules and new opportunities. Individuals have more choices than ever and better tools to help them choose. Time management is not always easy, but again there are tools to help you. It is a time for action, not complacency.

The New Normal is also a time of great challenges. For all of the progress technology offers us, there still are too many human problems it cannot fix. As I write these words, I am horrified by the reports from Iraq, troubled by the never-ending threat of terrorist attacks, frustrated that our leaders are incapable of moving us closer to peace. But like it or not, this is the time we live in. It is the New Normal. Some may complain, but the smart people will be those who make the best of a dynamic environment. Life today is wide open. It is wide open for so many people. I recommend that you dive in headfirst. Embrace the inevitable.

As you move forward, remember the secrets of the New Normal.

Choice—perceived by many as a burden—is a foundation of the New Normal. Priorities allow you to get past the nonessential choices, whereas focus enables you to make the right decision at the right time.

Individuals—freed of the protective cocoon of bureaucratic hierarchies—have more power than ever. You have increasing control of your life. All you have to do is take advantage of it.

Technology—once portrayed in movies and literature as dehumanizing—has become central to our everyday lives. It's bringing us closer to each other, expanding our access and our reach, helping us grow in ways that were unthinkable a couple of decades ago.

Globalization—often criticized for its imperfections—has expanded the economic pie. In the process it has increased stability in the world by bringing the most populous countries into the global economic fabric.

Time—the ever-shrinking fourth dimension—is now a secret weapon for individuals who know how to use it.

Yes, the world is far from perfect, and plagued by uncertainty, but I can't help but feel optimistic. We have at our fingertips the tools to improve our world. We just have to have the confidence to use them.

We can listen to pundits bent on scaring us into paralysis. Or we can ignore the doomsday machine. We can take charge.

Some might suggest it is my nature to forge optimistically into new territory: to start a new investment fund when others might begin winding down toward retirement, to devote so many of my waking hours to improving my guitar skills at an age that's about three decades after most musicians have given up and moved on to something else. Whatever it is, I don't have a patent on it. Anyone can do it.

The New Normal is about taking chances: knowing the risks, but taking advantage of opportunities that are within our grasp.

Be thoughtful. Work hard. Act. Have fun.

This is the New Normal. Make it yours.

INDEX